9

'020

the modern
VEGETARIAN

MARIA ELIA was born into the restaurant business – growing up in the kitchen of her Greek Cypriot father's restaurant in Richmond where, even at a really young age, she knew she wanted to be a chef herself.

After an apprenticeship at *Café Royal's Grill Room,* Maria's love of cooking has taken her around the world. She has worked in Italy, America and Australia, spent time cooking at *El Bulli* and *Arzak* restaurants in Spain and at *The Oriental Cooking School* in Bangkok. The regional flavours of all these far-flung places feature in Maria's recipes with considerable originality and earned her many fans during her 10-year tenure as head chef at the *Delfina Studio Café.*

Now a regular on BBC's *Ready Steady Cook,* Maria Elia was voted one of the Top 10 Female Chefs to watch by the *Independent.* She has also appeared on ITV's *Saturday Cooks, Daily Cooks* and BBC's *Food Poker* and writes for *Food and Travel, Olive* and *Waitrose Food Illustrated.*

the modern
VEGETARIAN

Food adventures for the contemporary palate

MARIA ELIA

Photography by Jonathan Gregson

Kyle Cathie Limited

First published in Great Britain in 2009 by

Kyle Cathie Limited

122 Arlington Road

London NW1 7HP

general.enquiries@kyle-cathie.com

www.kylecathie.com

ISBN 978 1 85626 820 2

10 9 8 7 6 5 4 3 2 1

Project editor Danielle Di Michiel
Designed by Jane Humphrey
Home economy by Annie Rigg (Annie Nichols on pp 17, 41, 47, 71,
81, 131 and 143)
Styling by Liz Belton
Production by Sha Huxtable

Maria Elia is hereby identified as the author of this work in
accordance with Section 77 of the Copyright, Designs and Patents
Act 1988.

A Cataloguing in Publication record for this title is available from
the British Library.

Colour reproduction by Sang Choy
Printed and bound in China by C & C Offset Printing Company Ltd

contents

introduction I have created a book where the vegetables are the 'heroes'. It is full of sensational flavours, colours, textures and taste adventures. Just because you've made a choice to omit or decrease meat or fish from your diet doesn't mean you necessarily have inactive taste buds! I feel vegetarians are often treated with contempt. For instance, as much as I love a mushroom risotto or a mozzarella, tomato and basil salad, I am always amused to see how many restaurants only offer these dishes as their vegetarian choice. As a chef, I've always ensured that there are enticing vegetarian dishes on my menus. Many of them appear here in this book, with not a 'nut loaf' in sight. It will appeal to vegetarians, carnivores and pescetarians alike. In fact, I hope this book inspires you whether you're a vegetarian or simply someone who wants to add more vegetables to your diet.

A recipe is so much more than a list of ingredients, it's about bringing those ingredients together in harmony and letting them come alive to reveal their diverse flavours and textures, in all their glorious simplicity or complexity. For example the 'textures of' peas, and beetroot and coffee sections that appear here are a collection of recipes that really take that ingredient 'out of the box' and show it in its many different guises.

Travel is a major inspiration: I've worked in Italy, the USA, Australia and Spain, as well as on a private yacht that travelled the world. I still travel as much as work permits, always to a country that promises to excite my palate and to offer new ideas with which I can experiment. Over the years I've worked with Michelin-starred French cuisine, Greek, Italian and everything in between. Now I refuse to be constrained by one particular style or cuisine. I prefer to find my own way. I live by this simple rule: food must stimulate the senses, looking and tasting fantastic.

Each season brings a host of new flavours which can be celebrated in recipes, both savoury and sweet. Working with ingredients in season is really so important, not only will they taste better and cost less, but they will also be at their most nutritious and plentiful. For me, there's nothing more exciting than the first strawberry crop. Although farmers' markets have done wonders in educating us on the importance of seasons, how many people honestly know the true pleasure of 'pick your own' strawberries compared with the anonymous kind bought in punnets from the local supermarket? If a fruit or vegetable that you thought of using is out of season, pick another recipe that embraces the fresh produce that is around. Or simply make a substitute in your recipe, it's easy once you have learnt to be brave enough to think creatively. I have suggested many substitutes in the introductions to the recipes that follow.

Ultimately cooking should be fun and come from the heart; it should bring pleasure and stimulate the senses and provide you with the pleasure of self-satisfaction. Everything is adaptable; sometimes the best results are created through improvisation. These recipes are simply building blocks by which you can build your own collection of delectable dishes. So, go on your own culinary journey and experiment along the way. Never be wed to the outcome and you will be delighted by what transpires – a bit like life really – you could be totally surprised!

Just relax, enjoy and get cooking, the results will taste so much better!

A note on cheese:

Cheese is much loved by vegetarians and a very useful, protein-rich alternative to meat. However, it is important to note that a large number of cheeses do contain unfamiliar animal ingredients, such as rennet, and are therefore not strictly suitable for a vegetarian diet.

However, the good news is that many cheeses are not made with this product; 65 per cent of all feta and halloumi is vegetarian, for example, as there is also a type of rennet that is derived from plants and bacteria, and used in vegetarian Parmesan, Cheddar, Gorgonzola, mozzarella and many many more. These products are almost always labelled with a vegetarian symbol and are vegetarian society-approved. When I refer to cheese as an ingredient in a recipe I give the name of the cheese but leave it up to you to decide which type of product will suit your preference. If you have any doubt, check the label or ask your friendly cheesemonger for advice.

SOPHISTICATED starters

CARROT PANCAKES WITH HOUMOUS AND A FETA SALAD

This recipe is perfect as a light lunch, snack or starter. It also makes great party canapés, as it can be prepared in advance. serves 4

For the pancakes

150g carrots, grated

1 small onion, finely chopped

2 green chillies, deseeded and finely chopped

2 teaspoons cumin seeds

1 teaspoon fennel seeds

2 teaspoons ground coriander

2 tablespoons chopped coriander

1 teaspoon baking powder

100g chickpea flour (or besan or gram flour)

50g semolina

2 teaspoons salt

150–200ml water

3 tablespoons olive oil, for frying

For the houmous

200g carrots, peeled

4 tablespoons olive oil

pinch of sea salt and freshly ground black pepper

200g chickpeas, cooked (tinned will do)

1 garlic clove, finely chopped

juice of half a lemon

2 tablespoons tahini

1 teaspoon ground cumin

For the salad

a bunch of watercress, thick stems removed

1 orange, peel and pith removed, cut into segments

1 punnet shiso (or any micro) sprouts

1 punnet coriander sprouts (or coriander leaf)

12 mint leaves, torn

50g alfalfa shoots

25g flaked almonds, toasted

pinch of ground cinnamon

50g feta cheese, crumbled

For the dressing

25ml sherry vinegar

25ml water

2 tablespoons extra virgin olive oil

1 teaspoon Dijon mustard

pinch of sugar

1 garlic clove, crushed

Preheat the oven to 200°C/400°F/Gas Mark 6.

To make the pancakes, mix all the ingredients, except the olive oil, together to form a thick batter. Heat the oil in a small non-stick frying pan until hot, then spoon in a quarter of the batter and fry until golden on both sides. Repeat with the remaining mixture to make 4 pancakes in total. Leave to cool on a wire rack.

Cut the carrots into thin slices, drizzle with olive oil and season with salt and pepper. Place on a baking tray and roast for about 20 minutes or until softened. While still hot, put them in a blender with the remaining ingredients and whizz to a smooth purée, adding a little water if too thick. Season again if necessary and refrigerate until needed. If you prefer, you can boil the carrots instead; just cook until tender and follow the recipe as above.

To make the salad, mix all of the salad ingredients and toss together well. Whisk the dressing ingredients together and season to taste. To assemble the dish, reheat the pancakes in a warm oven, place on individual plates and top with the carrot houmous. Dress the salad with the sherry dressing and place on top of the houmous.

ROSEMARY PORCINI

Porcini, for me, are the God of all mushrooms – rich, heady, meaty, velvety and sensationally delicious. Once a year I try to book a trip to Italy so that I can enjoy them at their best. Their season is summer to autumn and, although they are good dried, there is nothing quite like fresh ones. If you can't get hold of porcinis, use an interesting mix of farmed or wild mushrooms.

Serve with White Bean Truffle Purée (see p. 151) and griddled bread for a delicious light lunch or starter.
serves 4

600g porcini or mixed mushrooms

3 tablespoons extra virgin olive oil

1 garlic clove, finely chopped

2 sprigs of rosemary, picked, finely chopped

4 sage leaves, finely chopped

sea salt and black pepper

1 tablespoon red wine vinegar, preferably Cabernet Sauvignon

Wipe the mushrooms clean with a damp cloth and cut into rough 0.5cm slices. (Try to keep the slices a similar size so that they will all cook evenly.)

Heat half the oil in a large frying pan and add half the mushrooms, or just enough to cover the base. (Over-crowding the pan will cause the temperature to drop and the mushrooms will end up steaming rather than frying. That would be sacrilege!) Cook over a high heat for 3 minutes. Toss the pan, add half the garlic and herbs and a good pinch of salt and pepper and cook for a further 2 minutes, until coloured and tender.

Set aside and repeat with the remaining mushrooms, garlic and herbs, finishing this second batch with a dash of red wine vinegar.

Mix with the previously cooked mushrooms and serve as suggested above.

note To serve this recipe as a dinner party starter, try threading the mushroom caps onto sprigs of rosemary – remove the leaves from the bottom two thirds of each sprig and skewer mushrooms on to the end (you will probably need 4 large sprigs or 8 small ones). Cook as above, omitting the extra rosemary (you could pre-sear and finish in the oven or under the grill to save time).

CHILLI-ROASTED FETA AND WATERMELON SLAB

I absolutely adore watermelon. What could be more refreshing on a hot summer's day? I have childhood memories of my dad arriving home each evening with a vanload of watermelons, as they were his sideline in the summer after he gave up the restaurant.

The contrasts in this recipe are wonderful; I love the warmth of the feta and the heat from the chilli against the cold, sweet watermelon. The dressing is great with white beans, crumbled feta and some summery lettuce leaves. Or, if you prefer to keep it simple, just use a little lemon-infused olive oil to dress the watermelon. Perfect as a starter or light lunch. serves 4

4 evenly sized blocks of feta cheese
    (approximately 70g each)
extra virgin olive oil
1 teaspoon chilli flakes
1 punnet coriander sprouts (optional – if
    unavailable use coriander leaf)
1 punnet shiso sprouts (optional)

50g mizuna or baby salad leaves
25g toasted pine nuts (optional)
Raisin and Oregano Dressing (see p. 152)
4 pieces watermelon, cut into slightly larger
    rectangles than the feta, each approximately
    1.5cm high and chilled
olive oil, for drizzling

Preheat the oven to 190°C/375°F/Gas Mark 5.

Cut a large piece of foil and put it on a baking tray. Place each piece of feta on top, drizzle each piece with olive oil and sprinkle with a few chilli flakes. Put another piece of foil on top and fold the foil edges together to form a loose parcel. Place in the oven and cook for 8 minutes, by which time the feta will be soft and warm. (You can prepare the feta in advance but if you take it straight from the fridge you will need to double the cooking time.)

Remove from the oven and assemble immediately: Snip the coriander and shiso sprouts (if using) and mix with the baby leaves and pine nuts (if using). Dress with a little of the Raisin and Oregano Dressing and pile neatly on top of the chilled watermelon slabs.

Open the foil parcel and place the roasted feta on top of the salad leaves. Drizzle with olive oil and serve immediately.

FIG TARTE TATIN WITH SHAVED MANCHEGO AND ROCKET

Traditionally, Tarte Tatin is a dessert made from apples. This version, however, uses less sugar and vinegar to produce a 'tarter' taste which, together with the figs and sharpness of the manchego, creates a sensational mix of flavours, spiced up with peppery rocket.

You can also try this recipe with half-roasted plum tomatoes, whole cherry vines, cooked artichoke hearts, roasted fennel quarters or cooked quinces – they all work equally well. Try changing the cheese, too; a blue works beautifully with figs, as does pecorino. Another idea is to reduce some balsamic vinegar to a syrup over a low heat (don't refrigerate this, as it will set) and drizzle over the tarts – it's fantastic!

You will need blini pans for this. Blini pans are mini frying pans traditionally made from cast iron, about 12cm in diameter. There are some great non-stick varieties widely available. makes *4 blini-sized tarts*

1 sheet puff pastry (approximately 500g)
4 tablespoons caster sugar
2 tablespoons red wine vinegar, preferably Cabernet Sauvignon
1 tablespoon fresh thyme, chopped
8 figs

60g manchego, shaved
40g rocket leaves
olive oil, for drizzling
black pepper

Preheat the oven to 190°C/375°F/Gas Mark 5.

Roll out the pastry thinly and cut into 4 circles, slightly larger than the blini pans (approximately 15cm). Perforate all over with a fork and chill in the fridge until ready to use.

Put the sugar in a pan with a dash of water. Allow the mixture to boil until a nut-brown caramel forms, then remove from the heat.

Carefully add the vinegar and thyme and pour the caramel into 4 blini tins.

Cut the figs in half lengthways and place 4 halves in each pan, cut side down. Lay a pastry circle on each, tucking in the edges. Place on an oven tray and cook for about 20 minutes, or until the pastry is golden and puffed.

Remove from the oven and leave for a few minutes before inverting each one onto a flat plate.

Top with shaved manchego, drizzle with olive oil and season with black pepper.

SHAVED PORCINI AND FENNEL SALAD WITH VANILLA OIL

I do have an obsession with porcini. Here they are used in their simplest form – raw, creamy and pungent, tossed with vanilla oil, some crisp fennel and a few chives. If porcini are out of season, you can use good-quality frozen ones instead of fresh.

This simple salad makes a great dinner party starter that's light, yet has a full-on flavour. Make the vanilla oil up to two weeks in advance, and any leftovers can be tossed with some heritage tomatoes and a splash of white balsamic vinegar, or drizzled over griddled stone fruits.

This salad makes a great accompaniment for the White Bean Truffle Purée on p. 151, served on a bruschetta for a light lunch. serves *4*

For the vanilla oil
3 vanilla beans
250ml light olive oil

For the salad
I small fennel bulb
3 tablespoons freshly squeezed lemon juice
150g fresh porcini, wiped clean, very finely sliced
4 chives, finely sliced
sea salt and black pepper

To make the vanilla oil, split the vanilla beans in half lengthways and, using the back of a knife, scrape the seeds from the beans. Place the seeds, oil and beans in a small container and either whisk together or cover and shake well. Set aside, covered, for at least 2 days to infuse before using.

To make the salad, halve the fennel bulb lengthways, remove the core and finely slice across, using a sharp knife or mandolin. Place in a bowl and toss with the lemon juice. Add the remaining ingredients and 8 tablespoons of vanilla oil, season with sea salt and black pepper and carefully toss together.

Divide between 4 plates and serve chilled.

SWEETCORN POLENTA WITH ASPARAGUS AND SHIITAKE MUSHROOMS

A great way of using fresh sweetcorn for a sensational supper or starter. If corn is out of season, try making it with frozen corn. We used to serve this as a starter in the restaurant and it was always hugely popular. Try serving it with some patty pan squash or tenderstem broccoli instead of asparagus and shiitakes. serves 4

For the polenta

1 teaspoon sea salt

1 corn cob, leaves removed

75g instant polenta

25g butter

salt and pepper

1 tablespoon olive oil

For the cream of corn

1 corn cob

25g butter

2 shallots, finely chopped

1 garlic clove, finely chopped

pinch of nutmeg

sea salt and pepper

250ml double cream

For the accompaniments

8 spears of asparagus, roasted or steamed

160g shiitake mushrooms, sliced and sautéed

1 serving Sage Burnt Butter (see p. 160)

To make the polenta, bring a large pan of water to the boil, add the salt and the corn cob and cook until tender. Remove the corn and when cool enough to handle cut away the kernels from the cob (by holding it upright and slicing down the sides with a sharp knife). Set aside.

Measure the cooking water from the corn and make up 400ml. Return the pan to the heat and bring to the boil, then reduce the heat and slowly sprinkle in the polenta with one hand, whisking with the other. Cook over a low heat, stirring continuously until thickened. Stir in the butter and corn, check seasoning and pour into a baking tray (approximately 10 x 7cm) lined with plastic film; smooth the surface and set aside for about 40 minutes.

Preheat the oven to 220°C/425°F/Gas Mark 7.

Turn the polenta out onto a chopping board and cut into 4 even-sized pieces. Place the polenta on a non-stick baking tray, drizzle with olive oil and cook in the preheated oven for 15–20 minutes, until golden and hot in the centre.

To make the cream of corn, cut the kernels from the cob. Melt the butter in a saucepan over a medium heat, add the shallots and cook until tender, stirring occasionally. Add the garlic, nutmeg and corn, season with sea salt and pepper and cook for 1 minute. Add the cream, reduce the heat and simmer until the corn is tender (approximately 30 minutes), stirring occasionally. Purée until smooth and thick and check the seasoning.

To assemble, place a portion of polenta on each plate, top with a generous spoonful of warm cream of corn, followed by asparagus, shiitakes and then Sage Burnt Butter.

JERUSALEM ARTICHOKE BLINIS TOPPED WITH BLUE CHEESE

This dish was on the menu at Delfina's (the restaurant at which I was head chef) and it was extremely popular – a blessing, because the blinis are so easy to make and can be prepared in advance, gently reheated in the oven.

I like to use blu di Capra for this – an Italian blue-veined goat's cheese from the Piedmont area – but gorgonzola, dolcelatte or stichelton (a wonderful English blue, based on stilton) work really well too. If blue cheese is not your thing, try pecorino, a goat's cheese or manchego.

Parsnips can be used in place of artichokes for the blinis or, if you dislike both, you could simply use potatoes. And they're great topped with a poached egg. makes *8 blinis*

For the blinis

350g potatoes, peeled and cut into chunks

400g Jerusalem artichokes, peeled and cut
into chunks

100g plain flour

80ml double cream

2 teaspoons Dijon mustard

2 teaspoons chopped rosemary

4 eggs, separated

salt and black pepper

50g butter

400g blue cheese, sliced into 8 pieces

For the roasted artichokes

1 tablespoons olive oil

25g butter

250g Jerusalem artichokes, cut into wedges

salt and black pepper

For the dressing

100ml olive oil

35ml white wine vinegar, preferably Chardonnay

1 tablespoon clear honey

To serve

100g seasonal baby mixed leaves

1 pear, halved, cored and sliced

To make the blinis, cook the potatoes and artichokes separately in boiling salted water until soft. Strain and pass both through a fine sieve/ricer or mouli. Leave to cool. Add the flour, cream, mustard, rosemary and beaten egg yolks to the artichoke mix. Whisk the egg whites until soft peaks form, then fold into the artichoke mix. Season with salt and black pepper.

Heat the blini pans, add a little butter and then spoon in some of the blini mix. Cook over a medium heat for about 2 minutes on each side and repeat with the rest of the blini mixture.

Preheat the oven or grill to hot. Place a slice of cheese on top of each blini and put in the oven or under the grill until melted.

To prepare the roasted artichokes, heat a large frying pan until very hot. Add the olive oil and butter and carefully add the artichokes. Season with salt and black pepper and cook over a high heat until golden and tender. (If you have some fresh thyme add some picked leaves or chopped rosemary when cooking.)

To make the dressing, whisk together the olive oil, vinegar and honey. To assemble, toss the mixed leaves and pear in the dressing, scatter the artichokes over the cheese and pile the mixed leaves and pear on top. Serve immediately.

ROQUEFORT AND FIG CRÈME BRÛLÉE WITH A PECAN SALAD

This is a luxurious, creamy brûlée, topped with crushed, peppered pecan nuts, and is great as a light lunch/starter or as an alternative cheese course, served with a glass of Sauternes. Serve with rustic grissini (breadsticks) or toast, as shown in the picture opposite, and with a pear and pecan salad. As a variation, you could replace the Roquefort with a Stilton (such as a Colston Bassett), substitute seedless grapes for the figs or even omit the fruit and use some sautéed leeks or diced roast beetroot instead.   serves 6

For the crème brûlée
500ml double cream
2 garlic cloves, halved
5 egg yolks
25g caster sugar
1 teaspoon sea salt
large pinch of white pepper
200g Roquefort cheese, crumbled
4 dried figs, soaked in hot water for 10 minutes,
  drained and cut into small dice
4 tablespoons demerara sugar
12 grissini (breadsticks)

25g pecan nuts, roasted
cracked black pepper
For the pear and pecan salad
1 pear, cored and sliced
100g mixed baby salad leaves
25g pecan nuts
4 pickled green figs, quartered, or 2 fresh
  figs (optional)
For the dressing
20ml light olive oil
20ml extra virgin olive oil
20ml white wine or Chardonnay vinegar

Preheat the oven to 150°C/300°F/Gas Mark 2. Heat the cream and garlic in a pan.

Whisk the egg yolks, sugar, salt and white pepper together until pale. Slowly whisk a little of the hot cream into the yolks, then add the remaining cream and strain through a sieve into a bowl. Stir in half the Roquefort cheese.

Divide the dried figs and the remaining Roquefort between 6 ramekins and fill each one with the cream mixture. Place the ramekins in a baking tin lined with a tea towel and fill with enough hot water to reach halfway up the sides of the ramekins. Cook in the oven for about 30–50 minutes, or until set (this will depend on the size of the ramekins). Leave to cool and then chill in the fridge for at least 2 hours.

Top the brûlées with the demerara sugar and blast them with a blowtorch or under a very hot grill until caramelised. Skewer the brûlées immediately with a couple of grissini broken to different lengths, then mix the pecans with cracked black pepper and sprinkle over the top.

To make the salad, mix together the pears, mixed leaves, pecans and pickled figs (if using). Whisk the oils and vinegar together and use to dress the salad. Serve with the Roquefort crème brûlées.

note If you don't own a blowtorch, try heating a metal dessertspoon in a gas flame until it is red hot then, using the back of the spoon, carefully caramelise the sugar. The spoon will never be the same again, but your crème brûlées will look great!

textures of peas

textures of peas I get so excited about summer produce. My flatmate is training to be a gardener and every spring she plants pots of peas, runner beans, aubergines, carrots, cherry tomatoes, lettuces and courgettes, so our garden is full of tubs of fresh herbs, making us pretty much self-sufficient in the summer. This section embraces the pea! Most people discard the pod, but with just a little water and a few mint and basil stalks you can make a beautiful pea stock.

'Textures of Peas' demonstrates the extraordinary potential of the humble pea. Here are five innovative ways to make the most of your peas: savoury pea 'custard' served cold; a chilled pea jelly; a hot mint, basil and pea soup; a few pea shoots and peas steamed in their pods. You can impress dinner guests by serving it all together as a selection of 'tasters' (as we have in the picture, left) or, if that sounds too much, just make a part of the recipe.

FRESH PEA STOCK

Mostly, pea pods are consigned to the bin or the compost heap, but they can make a beautiful, simple stock that is perfect for use in the Pea, Basil and Mint Soup (see p. 31) or in a risotto.

500g fresh pea pods
1 shallot, peeled and finely sliced

stalks of a bunch each of mint and basil
salt and pepper

Wash the pea pods and place in a saucepan with the shallot and herb stalks. Cover with water and bring to the boil, then simmer for 30–40 minutes only. Season to taste, then pass through a fine sieve. (For a stronger flavour, reduce by one third, boiling the stock again after you have sieved it.)

Leave to cool and either chill in the fridge or freeze until required.

SWEET PEA CUSTARDS

makes *If you're making this along with the other pea recipes in the 'Textures of Peas' series, it makes 8 small 'taster' ramekins. If you're eating it on its own, it will make 4 ramekins*

350g fresh or frozen peas (podded weight);   **1 teaspoon lemon juice**
    reserve the pods for stock   **sea salt and pepper**
a handful of mint leaves   **oil, for greasing**
3 eggs   **pea shoots, for garnishing**
160ml double cream

Preheat the oven to 180°C/350°F/Gas Mark 4.

Put the kettle and a large pot of salted water on to boil. In a pan, blanch the peas for 5 minutes or until tender, add the mint leaves and cook for 30 seconds. Drain and refresh the peas and mint in cold water (this helps to keep their colour). Drain then whizz in a blender to a purée, together with the eggs, cream and lemon juice, until very smooth. Season with sea salt and pepper.

Grease the ramekins with a little oil and divide the custard mixture between them. Place a kitchen towel on the base of a small baking tin, sitting the ramekins on top (this will prevent them from sliding around). Fill with enough hot water from the kettle to go halfway up the sides of the ramekins, cover with foil and cook for 25–30 minutes or until just set. Remove foil and leave to cool in the tin. Chill in the fridge until required, then run a knife around the edge of each custard, slip them out onto plates and serve with some hot pea soup and pea jelly.

To serve the custards as a light lunch, they would be delicious accompanied by a pea shoot, basil, mint and baby spinach salad; some crumbled feta cheese and cooked broccoli spears would also be great.

PEA, BASIL AND MINT SOUP

It might seem odd that I'm advocating using frozen peas for this recipe, but the reason is for their colour. Adding a third of the peas at the end will result in a bright pea-green colour that is virtually impossible to achieve with fresh peas. (You could also use a mixture of fresh and frozen peas, leaving the frozen third to the end.)

This soup can be served hot, but is equally delicious served chilled. serves *4 or 8 'textures of peas' tasters*

1 tablespoon olive oil
1 small white onion, peeled, finely chopped
500g frozen petit pois peas
600ml hot Fresh Pea Stock (see p. 29) or water
half a small bunch of mint, leaves picked (stalks reserved for stock)

a small bunch of basil, leaves picked (stalks reserved for stock)
pinch of white sugar
1 teaspoon sea salt

Heat the oil in a medium-sized saucepan. Add the onion until softened and translucent. Add two thirds of the peas, the stock or water, half the mint and basil and the sugar and salt. Bring to the boil, then simmer for 20 minutes or until the peas are tender.

Put the soup in a blender in batches, adding the remaining peas and herbs, and whiz to a smooth purée. Adjust the seasoning to taste and serve.

note Sorrel works beautifully with peas – try using it here instead of the herbs for a lovely lemony flavour. If you are serving this soup on its own, you might want to try adding some cooked peas, torn mint, crumbled feta or tofu, crème fraîche or Pea Jelly (see p. 32) as a garnish.

PEA JELLY

An interesting savoury jelly that can be used to top bruschetta, along with crème fraîche and asparagus spears or as a garnish for Chilled Pea Soup. serves *4 or 8 as a 'Textures of Peas'*

150ml Fresh Pea Stock (see p.29) or water
pinch of salt
125g fresh or frozen peas (podded weight)
15g butter
1 small shallot, finely diced

2 tablespoons chopped tarragon
20ml cream
1.5g agar agar powder
salt and pepper

Bring the pea stock or water to the boil, add a pinch of salt and cook the peas until tender. Drain the peas, reserving the cooking liquor.

Heat the butter in a small pan, add the shallot and cook until softened and translucent. Add the peas, tarragon and cream and simmer for 4 minutes.

Measure the reserved cooking liquor and make it up to 150ml again, if necessary, with water. Return the cooking liquor to the heat, whisk in the agar agar and simmer for 2 minutes. Pour the two mixtures into a blender and whizz until smooth. Pass through a sieve and season with salt and pepper.

Pour into a shallow plastic container and leave to cool before refrigerating. Refrigerate until set (about 1 hour) then cut into cubes and serve with pea custards etc.

If you are making the pea soup and serving it chilled, try using this jelly as a garnish. It also makes a great canapé, served on teaspoons and topped with crème fraîche, finely grated lemon zest and a pea shoot. Alternatively, top with a slice of soft goat's cheese, or, if you want to be really flash, pour a little jelly into the base of some shot glasses and top when set with a little chilled pea soup and crème fraîche. To assemble 'Textures of Peas' you will need 4 pea pods (steamed or blanched for a minute and popped open) and some pea shoots to garnish.

SMASHED PEA, DILL AND FETA CROSTINI

A Greek-style crostini, taking advantage of summer sweet peas, lovely with salty feta, refreshing lemon and dill. Serve as part of 'Textures of Peas'. serves 4. *If making as 'Textures of Peas', halve the bread to give 8 pieces.*

1 garlic clove

2 tablespoons of fresh dill, finely chopped

sea salt

150g fresh peas (podded weight)

5 tablespoons olive oil

100g feta cheese, crumbled

25g freshly grated Parmesan cheese (optional)

2 tablespoons lemon juice

pepper

4 slices mini ciabatta

pea shoots, to garnish

Place the garlic and dill in a pestle and mortar with a pinch of sea salt, pound until crushed and transfer to a bowl.

Working in batches, smash the peas in the pestle and mortar with a pinch of salt and a little of the olive oil until paste-like. Mix with the garlic and dill, feta and Parmesan (if using) and dress with the lemon juice and remaining olive oil. Season to taste if necessary.

Preheat a griddle pan and toast the bread on both sides until golden. Top the ciabatta slices with the smashed peas and garnish with pea shoots.

CHILLED TOMATO, PEACH AND GINGER SOUP

The combination of tomato and peach is delicious. Jazzed up with warming ginger and a hint of red chilli it makes the perfect summer soup, and is one of my favourites. Serve it with some Thai basil (Italian works too), a little diced tomato and peach and a drizzle of olive oil, and you're sure to impress! serves 4

4 tablespoons olive oil, plus extra for drizzling

2 large shallots (or 8 small), peeled, halved
  lengthways and finely sliced

70g fresh ginger, peeled and finely sliced

1kg plum vine tomatoes

8 ripe peaches

4 garlic cloves, finely sliced

1 red chilli, split in half lengthways

pinch of white sugar

sea salt and pepper

8 Thai basil leaves, torn

Heat the olive oil in a saucepan over a medium heat. Add the shallots and ginger and cook over a medium-low heat until 'caramelised' (sticky and softened) – this will take about 15 minutes.

Meanwhile, bring a large pan of water (or a kettle) to the boil. Remove the core and lightly criss cross the base of each tomato with a knife. Put them in a large bowl, pour hot water over them and leave for 30 seconds. Drain and set aside. Repeat with the peaches, but leave for about 1 minute or until the skins begin to loosen. Remove and discard skins from peaches and tomatoes and set aside one of each for the garnish. Add the garlic and chilli to the shallots and cook for a further 5 minutes.

Roughly chop the tomatoes, reserving all the juices, and add to the pan. Roughly chop the peaches, discarding the stones and add to the pan. Add the sugar, sea salt and 650ml water and bring to the boil, then reduce the heat and simmer for 30 minutes.

Meanwhile, prepare the garnish. Cut the reserved tomato in half, lengthways, then into quarters and remove the seeds (adding to the soup). Cut each tomato 'petal' into ½-cm dice. Repeat with the reserved peach. Refrigerate until required.

Remove and discard the chilli from the soup. Purée the soup until smooth (add a little water if too thick), season to taste, cool and then refrigerate, covered, until required.

Serve garnished with peach and tomato dice, Thai basil leaves and a drizzle of olive oil.

note If you are feeling adventurous you could also try garnishing with a little deep-fried ginger. You will need a long piece of ginger (I say long, as this means your fingers will be further away from the blade!), which you peel, then using a very sharp knife or mandolin, slice into wafer-thin pieces. Heat a small pan of vegetable oil until almost smoking and fry the ginger in batches until golden. Remove and drain on kitchen paper. These ginger crisps can also be made in advance and stored in an airtight container.

WATERMELON GAZPACHO – THAI STYLE

I've always felt more than comfortable with Middle Eastern, Moroccan, Spanish and Italian flavours (largely, I think, because of my Greek background) and, before I spent eight weeks travelling around Thailand, Thai cooking was, for me, uncharted territory. So I booked myself on a cooking course at the Oriental Hotel and another in Chang Mai and this marked a turning point in my culinary career.

I discovered the use of sweet, salty, sour and hot ingredients with flavour sensations such as I'd never experienced before – so pure, clean and refreshing, almost stopping you in your tracks as they 'pop' in the mouth. This is a no-cook soup that's quick and easy to make ahead of time and perfect for a summer dinner party in the garden. serves 4

1 litre watermelon juice

2 plum vine tomatoes, peeled and roughly
   chopped

2 sticks lemongrass, finely chopped

3cm fresh ginger, peeled and grated

1 garlic clove, peeled and finely chopped

1 red chilli, finely chopped (leave the seeds in if
   you like it 'hot')

1 shallot, peeled and finely chopped

a small bunch of coriander, finely chopped

2 tablespoons extra virgin olive oil

juice of 1 lime

salt

For the garnish

4 tablespoons diced watermelon

1 avocado, finely diced

chopped coriander (reserved from soup
   quantity above)

4 mint leaves, torn

Blend together the watermelon juice, tomatoes, lemongrass, ginger, garlic, chilli and shallot until smooth. Add half the coriander, the olive oil and lime juice and whizz again until smooth. Season with salt and chill in the fridge (overnight if you like). Serve the gazpacho chilled and garnished with the diced watermelon, avocado and herbs.

note You could vary the garnish by adding some freshly grated coconut or some chopped cashew nuts, Vietnamese mint or Thai basil or some finely diced Granny Smith apple.

LEMONGRASS AND SWEETCORN SOUP WITH CRÈME FRAÎCHE

One Friday lunchtime at Delfina's we were extremely busy and, although it was a summer's day, there was an unexpected run on the soup! I knew there wouldn't be enough for the evening and there were no ingredients left to make more. Faced with such situations, I usually go to the walk-in fridge and look for possible ingredient combinations. On this particular occasion, my eye fell upon sweetcorn and lemongrass. I was saved and this soup was born!

Fresh, seasonal corn is best for this, but you can always use frozen or tinned if none is available. Cauliflower and lemongrass is also a wonderful combination – simply cut a small cauliflower into florets and follow the recipe as below. Then try roasting some thinly sliced florets in a hot oven and adding to the remaining relish ingredients. serves 4

3 corn cobs

50g butter

1 small white onion, finely chopped

3cm fresh ginger, peeled and finely chopped

1 red chilli, deseeded and finely chopped

25g plain flour

1 litre milk

5 sticks lemongrass, finely chopped

salt and pepper

4 tablespoons crème fraîche

Using a sharp knife, carefully cut the corn kernels from the cob. Set cobs and kernels aside.

Gently heat the butter. Add the onion, ginger and chilli and sauté until softened but not browned (about 5 minutes). Add the flour, stir and cook for 1 minute. Add the milk, lemongrass, corn and the cobs and stir, bringing to the boil. Reduce the heat and simmer for 20 minutes.

Discard the corn cobs and blend the soup in a food-processor until smooth, then pass through a sieve and season. Serve with a swirl of crème fraîche and Sweetcorn Relish (see p. 155).

TOMATO AND FIG SOUP WITH GOAT'S CHEESE BRUSCHETTA

I created this soup one October, when all the broad beans, peas and heritage tomatoes had finished and the thought of four months of root vegetables ahead was on my mind. I had a load of dried figs in the storeroom and a few tins of plum tomatoes and, with both being quite sweet ingredients, I used some lovely warming spices – cinnamon and cumin, with a hint of chilli – to bring them together nicely. A few onions and some garlic later, and a delicious soup was cooking.

When it comes to soups, I think a lot of people forget about the 'topping'. A crusty bruschetta topped with melting goat's cheese, a few slices of soaked dried figs and a bit of torn rocket make this soup into a decadent starter or a satisfying light lunch or supper. To bulk it out a little, you could throw in a few red lentils 20 minutes before the end of cooking, or add some chickpeas. If goat's cheese is not your thing, feta works equally well.

serves 6

For the soup

4 tablespoons olive oil

1 Spanish onion, finely sliced

2 garlic cloves, finely chopped

1 green pepper, finely sliced

2 teaspoons ground cumin

small pinch of chilli flakes

4cm cinnamon stick

3 bay leaves

1.5kg vine tomatoes, skinned and roughly
   chopped

50g caster sugar

100g dried figs, soaked in 700ml boiling water for
   20 minutes

sea salt and freshly ground black pepper

a handful of rocket leaves, to garnish

For the bruschetta

6 slices ciabatta bread, toasted

225g goat's cheese, thinly sliced

3 fresh figs, sliced

To make the soup, heat the olive oil in a large, heavy saucepan, add the onion, garlic and green pepper and cook until softened. Stir in the cumin, chilli flakes, cinnamon stick and bay leaves and continue to cook for a further 2 minutes. Add the tomatoes, sugar and figs (together with their soaking water) and simmer over a gentle heat for about 25 minutes. Discard the cinnamon stick and season with salt and pepper.

Blend the soup (with the bay leaves) in a liquidiser until smooth.

To make the bruschetta, top the toasted ciabatta slices with the thinly sliced goat's cheese and grill until the cheese is bubbling and golden. Cover with the fig slices.

To serve, garnish the hot soup with rocket leaves and accompany with the fig-topped bruschetta.

SPICED RED LENTIL, ORANGE AND GINGER SOUP

There is nothing more comforting than a bowl of this spicy, fragrant soup – one of my favourites – on a cold winter's day. And it tastes even better the next day – when all the flavours have had a chance to develop. I like to add a dash of Thai sweet chilli when I make this; the sweetness it brings to the soup and the extra spice are delicious. Try garnishing with crumbled feta and crispy fried onions as an alternative to yogurt. serves 4

250g red lentils

3 tablespoons olive oil

1 onion, finely chopped

1 celery stalk, finely chopped

1 carrot, peeled and finely diced

1 red chilli, deseeded and finely chopped

2 garlic cloves, peeled and finely chopped

50g fresh ginger, peeled and finely chopped
    or grated

4 teaspoons ground cumin

¼ teaspoon each of ground turmeric and paprika

pinch of cayenne pepper

2 vegetable bouillon cubes

1½ tablespoons tomato purée

2 cinnamon sticks

2 oranges

salt and pepper

4 tablespoons Greek yogurt

fresh mint leaves, to garnish

Put the lentils in a saucepan, cover with water, bring to the boil, drain in a fine-holed colander and rinse with cold water.

In a large saucepan, heat the olive oil, add the onion, celery, carrot, chilli, garlic and ginger and sauté over a medium heat for 5 minutes. Add the spices to the pan and cook for a further 2 minutes. Add the lentils, bouillon cubes, tomato purée, cinnamon sticks and 750ml of water.

Finely grate the orange zest from 1 orange, then top and tail both, remove the remaining skin and cut the flesh into small pieces. Add to the pan, along with the zest.

Bring to the boil, then reduce the heat to a gentle simmer and cook for about 30 minutes, stirring occasionally. You might need to add water to keep the mixture 'soupy'.

Cook until the lentils are tender then remove the cinnamon sticks and, using a hand blender, lightly blend the soup. Adjust the seasoning to taste and serve, topped with Greek yogurt and shredded mint leaves.

FENNEL, CARDAMOM AND COCONUT SOUP

I love fennel and find that its aniseed flavour is a perfect accompaniment to coconut. serves 4

2 tablespoons grapeseed oil

3 shallots, finely chopped

30g fresh ginger, peeled and finely chopped

1 garlic clove, finely chopped

2 green chillies, finely chopped

2 teaspoons fennel seeds

15 cardamom pods, crushed and husks
    removed

2 fennel bulbs (weighing about 500g),
    quartered and finely sliced

50ml Pernod (optional)

2 x 400ml tins coconut milk

2 tablespoons soy sauce

2 tablespoons lime juice

2 tablespoons Thai sweet chilli sauce

coriander leaves, to garnish

Heat the grapeseed oil in a large pan. Once the oil is hot add the shallots, ginger, garlic, chilli, fennel seeds and cardamom. Cook over a medium heat for 3 minutes. Add the fennel and Pernod (if using) and cook for 2 minutes or until most of the Pernod has evaporated. Add the coconut milk and 200ml of water. Bring to the boil. Reduce the heat to a simmer and cook for 10–15 minutes until the fennel is tender. Add the soy sauce, lime juice and sweet chilli. If the mixture is a bit too thick add a dash of water. Serve piping hot, garnished with a few coriander leaves.

SWEET POTATO AND COCONUT SOUP

On ITV's *Daily Cooks Challenge*, I, along with the other chefs, was always faced with the challenge of keeping our ingredients lists to a minimum. On one show, I got particularly lucky and was given sweet potato as an ingredient. With only two minutes to play with, I hit on the recipe below. Simple and delicious. serves 4

700g sweet potatoes

2 x 400ml tins coconut milk

1 tablespooon Thai red curry paste

dash of soy sauce

coriander, to garnish

Preheat the oven to 180°C/350°F/Gas Mark 4.

Roast the sweet potatoes for 40 minutes or until tender. Remove from the oven and leave to cool slightly. Then cut in half, scoop out the flesh and put in a blender.

Heat the coconut milk and curry paste and cook until aromatic. Whizz in the blender with the sweet potato until smooth, then season with soy sauce. Serve piping hot, garnished with coriander.

SENSATIONAL
mains

BUTTERNUT SQUASH TAGINE WITH BUTTERED CHILLI COUSCOUS

Here is my version of the amazing tagines I've had in Morocco. You can, of course, use any other variety of squash available or substitute carrots, turnips or courgettes. (The cooking times will vary slightly for each.) serves 4

1 medium-sized butternut squash	2 teaspoons coriander seeds, crushed
2 tablespoons olive oil	2 x 400g tins tomatoes, crushed by hand
1 onion, finely chopped	2 red chillies, split lengthways
2 garlic cloves, finely chopped	1 cinnamon stick
pinch of salt	1 tablespoon honey
pinch of saffron threads	500ml water
3 teaspoons ground cumin	sea salt and black pepper
1 teaspoon ground ginger	half a small bunch of coriander, finely chopped
2 teaspoons paprika	50g roasted flaked almonds, to garnish

Peel the butternut squash with a potato peeler. Cut in half widthways, then again lengthways, scoop out the seeds with a spoon, then cut into approximately 2cm chunks. Reserve the peel and trim for stock.

Heat the olive oil in a pan, sauté the onion until softened, add the garlic and all the dry spices and cook 'out' for 2 minutes, until fragrant. Add the tomatoes, chillies, cinnamon stick, honey and water and bring to the boil. Add the butternut squash, season with sea salt and black pepper and simmer for 30 minutes until the mixture has thickened and the squash is tender, adding more water if necessary. Stir in the coriander and adjust the seasoning. Sprinkle with almonds and serve with Buttered Chilli and Date Couscous (see below). And beware of the chillies!

BUTTERED CHILLI AND DATE COUSCOUS In Morocco, couscous is traditionally lovingly prepared in a couscoussière; it is an art form – a prolonged process of steaming and dredging. The result, however, is sublime! Here is my simple, quick version using instant couscous. serves 4

350g instant couscous	pinch of salt
50g butter, diced	350ml boiling water
finely grated zest of 1 lemon	75g dates, pitted, finely sliced
1 green chilli, deseeded and finely chopped	half a small bunch of coriander, finely chopped

Place the couscous, butter, lemon zest and chilli in a bowl. Add a pinch of salt and pour over boiling water. Cover with clingfilm and leave for 2–3 minutes to steam. Remove the clingfilm and fluff with a fork to loosen the couscous grains. Stir in the dates and coriander.

MUSHROOM, BEETROOT, MOZZARELLA WITH A LENTIL CARTOUCHE

Cartouche is Italian for 'parcel', and this recipe is so-called because it combines some great earthy flavours in one fabulous parcel.

I've used mozzarella for its creaminess, to temper the sharpness of the ginger vinaigrette, but pecorino works equally well. Asparagus could replace the beetroot, if preferred. And, if you don't fancy making the parcels, use the recipe as a salad instead. serves 4

For the ginger vinaigrette dressing

1cm piece ginger

1 garlic clove, finely grated

30ml rice vinegar

1 tablespoon soy sauce

1 tablespoon lemon juice

1 tablespoon sugar

75ml sesame oil

2 teaspoons Dijon mustard

For the lentils

225g puy or brown lentils

3 tablespoons olive oil

1 Spanish onion, finely chopped

2 garlic cloves, finely chopped

2 bay leaves

salt and pepper

4 tablespoons coriander leaves, chopped

For the mushroms

4 large Portobello mushrooms, or 8 small ones

2 tablespoons olive or sesame oil

salt

pinch of chilli flakes (optional)

To assemble

500g buffalo mozzarella cheese, torn into 4 pieces

200g cooked beetroot, cut into wedges

4 squares of parchment paper (approximately 38 x 38cm)

4 strips of parchment paper (approximately 38 x 2cm), to tie

Prepare the vinaigrette in advance by whisking all the ingredients together. Refrigerate until required.

For the lentils, wash them in a sieve under cold water. Heat the oil in a saucepan, add the onion and garlic and sauté over a medium heat until softened. Add the drained lentils, bay leaves and just enough water to cover. Bring to the boil and simmer until tender, about 15–20 minutes, adding more water if necessary. Drain the lentils and dress with the ginger vinaigrette while still hot. Season with salt and pepper and stir through the coriander.

To prepare the mushrooms, wipe the caps clean with a damp cloth and remove the stalks. Drizzle with the olive oil, season with salt and chilli flakes and cook in a preheated frying pan or griddle for 3 minutes on either side.

To assemble, preheat the oven to 190°C/375°F/Gas Mark 5. Place 1 mushroom (or 2, if small) in the centre of each paper square and top with lentils, mozzarella and beetroot wedges. Bring the sides of the squares together and tie each one with a strip. (All of this can be done in advance; the parcels will keep for 2 days in the fridge.) Place on a baking tray and cook for 15–20 minutes or until heated right through. Serve with a rocket salad.

CHESTNUT PASTA RAGS WITH SPROUTS AND WILD MUSHROOMS

These chestnut rags, or *stracci di castagne*, are mildly nutty in flavour. You can vary the dish by omitting the butter, drizzling with truffle oil and tossing with crushed, roasted hazelnuts for extra texture. I always salt the cooking water, rather than the pasta dough. serves 4

For the pasta

250g '00' flour

125g cooked chestnuts, whizzed to a fine powder

6 egg yolks

I whole egg

dash of olive oil

semolina, for dusting

For the vegetables

2 tablespoons olive oil

250g wild mushrooms, cleaned and torn

salt and pepper

250g Brussels sprouts, cooked

50g unsalted butter

150g cooked chestnuts, quartered

I serving Sage Burnt Butter (see p. 160)

50g Parmesan cheese, shaved

To make the pasta by hand, combine the flour and chestnuts on a work surface, form them into a mound and make a well in the centre. Add the eggs and oil and mix gradually until most of the flour is incorporated. Knead for about 10 minutes, or until the dough is firm and elastic, adding more flour if it is too sticky. Wrap in clingfilm and leave to rest for 30 minutes, during which time the dough will soften.

If you are using a food-processor, combine the flour and chestnuts, keep the motor running and slowly add the eggs and oil, mixing until it just comes together. (If you overwork the mixture it will heat up too much!) Transfer to a work surface and knead as above. Wrap in clingfilm, then chill in the fridge for I hour or overnight – the pasta will become much more flexible after resting. (If you own a KitchenAid, make the pasta using the dough hook attachment; this is what I do in the restaurant.)

Transfer the dough to a lightly floured surface and press gently to flatten. Cut in half and roll each piece of dough through a pasta machine several times starting at the thickest setting and ending at the thinnest. Cut into 5cm rough diamond-shaped rags (a pizza wheel is really good for this), place on a tray lined with baking paper and sprinkled with semolina and leave to rest for 10 minutes before cooking. You can complete this stage up to 3 days in advance. If you don't own a pasta machine, use a rolling pin, and cut into rags.

To prepare the vegetables, heat the olive oil in a large pan and cook the mushrooms over a high heat, seasoning with salt and pepper. Set aside.

Halve or quarter the Brussels sprouts, depending on their size. Heat the butter and warm the sprouts and chestnuts over a medium heat.

To serve, cook the pasta in a large pan of generously salted boiling water until al dente, 1–2 minutes. Toss the sprouts, mushrooms and chestnuts with the pasta rags in Sage Burnt Butter, season with sea salt and pepper and serve topped with shaved Parmesan.

RED BRAISED MUSHROOMS

Here, the red braising liquor is great for cooking any vegetables, such as aubergines, sweet potatoes or cabbage. My friend, the fantastic chef, Kim, introduced me to this.

In this one-pot aromatic dish, the mushrooms are braised with fried shallots, garlic, coriander root, chilli and ginger – the five key ingredients in any Asian-inspired dish. serves 4

For the red braising liquor

200ml soy sauce

200ml Shaoxing (Chinese Rice Wine, see p. 170)

150g yellow rock sugar (see p. 170)

2 strips dried Asian orange peel (or fresh, if unavailable)

I red chilli

a small bunch of coriander, roots attached

4cm fresh ginger, thinly sliced

2 cinnamon sticks

2 star anise

I litre water

For the mushrooms

a bunch of coriander, roots removed, finely chopped

2 tablespoons grapeseed or vegetable oil

2 garlic cloves, peeled and finely diced

2 shallots, finely diced

2cm fresh ginger, peeled and finely diced

I red chilli, deseeded and finely diced

400g mixed mushrooms (for example: 100g shiitakes, quartered; oyster mushrooms, torn in half; enoki mushrooms, cut from stems)

For the braise, place all the ingredients together in a large saucepan and bring to the boil. Simmer for 10 minutes. Strain and discard the aromatics.

Prepare the mushrooms. Remove the roots from the coriander, wash and finely chop. Heat the oil in a wok and stir-fry the garlic, shallots, ginger, chilli and the coriander roots for 2 minutes. Add the mushrooms and enough braising liquor to cover and simmer for 20 minutes, or until the mushrooms are tender. Finely chop the coriander and add to the mushrooms.

Serve in deep bowls with jasmine rice and a spoon. Alternatively, try with Salt and Pepper Tofu (see p. 113) and broccoli or Aubergine Relish (see p. 155) for a decadent dinner party dish.

RED LENTIL DHAL, AUBERGINE AND SPINACH STACK WITH RAITA

If you prepare the dhal and aubergines the day before (which is best, since they improve in flavour), this is a great recipe for entertaining or for a quick and easy supper. serves 4

2 medium aubergines

200ml olive oil

100ml lemon juice

Red Lentil Dhal (see p. 114)

2 handfuls of baby spinach leaves

a few mint and coriander sprigs and leaves

salt and pepper

Apple Raita (see p. 159)

4 cooked poppadoms, to garnish (optional)

Preheat the oven to 180°C/350°F/Gas Mark 4. Cut the aubergines lengthways into twelve 1cm-thick slices. Whisk the olive oil and lemon juice together and brush over either side of the slices. Place them on a non-stick baking tray and cook until tender, about 8 minutes. Reserve the remaining olive oil and lemon juice for dressing the spinach leaves.

To assemble, reheat the dhal and aubergines, toss the spinach leaves and herbs with the reserved lemon juice and olive oil, then season with salt and pepper. Place an aubergine slice on each plate, top with dhal, repeat with another layer and top with spinach. Place the remaining aubergine slices on top. Serve with a large spoonful of raita on the side of each plate and break each poppadom in 3, standing the pieces upright in the raita. Garnish with coriander sprigs.

WATERMELON CURRY WITH BLACK BEANS AND PANEER

This does sound unusual, but once you've tried it you'll probably be hooked. Refreshing and lightly spiced, this curry is great for the summer. Serve with paneer or replace with tofu. For a more spicy curry, leave the seeds in the chilli. You could also try adding some mixed tomato quarters to the curry during the last ten minutes of cooking. serves 4

3kg watermelon (seedless, if possible)

2 tablespoons grapeseed oil

1 large white onion, finely chopped

6cm fresh ginger, finely chopped or grated

3 garlic cloves, finely chopped

2 red chillies, deseeded and finely chopped

2 stalks lemongrass, finely chopped

2 teaspoons ground turmeric

4 teaspoons ground coriander

2 teaspoons cumin seeds

pinch of cayenne pepper

250g paneer, cut into 2cm cubes

1 x 400g tin cooked black beans, rinsed
   and drained

a small bunch of coriander, leaves finely chopped
   (and some sprigs, to garnish)

sea salt

juice of 1–2 limes, to taste

Slice the top and bottom off the watermelon, slice vertically in half, then cut again into quarters. Carefully remove the flesh from the skin and any seeds. Whizz 2.5kg of the watermelon in a blender or food processor until smooth. Dice the remaining 500g of watermelon into 1cm cubes and set aside.

Heat half the oil in a frying pan, add the onions, ginger and garlic and cook over a medium heat until softened. Add the chillies, lemongrass and spices and cook for a further minute, or until fragrant. Add the watermelon purée, bring to the boil, then simmer until reduced by half (about 20 minutes).

Meanwhile, heat the remaining oil in a frying pan, add the paneer and fry over a medium heat until golden. Remove with a slotted spoon and drain on kitchen paper.

Once the curry has reduced, stir in the beans and paneer, diced watermelon and coriander and season with a generous pinch of sea salt. Warm through and flavour with lime juice.

Serve with Coconut Basmati Rice (see p. 102) and garnished with coriander sprigs.

ARTICHOKE AND GOAT'S CHEESE RAVIOLI

A delicious artichoke ravioli recipe that uses ready-made wonton wrappers (you'll find these in your local Asian supermarket). I've used a blue goat's cheese here because it complements the artichokes (you could, of course, use a soft blue cow's milk cheese), while the Parmesan adds body. serves 4

For the ravioli

2 lemons, 1 juiced and 1 cut in half

2 bay leaves

2 garlic cloves, peeled and crushed

a few sprigs of fresh thyme

sea salt and black pepper

3 globe artichokes

300g soft blue goat's cheese

50g freshly grated Parmesan cheese

30g pine nuts, toasted

half a bunch of basil, finely chopped

20–24 square wonton skins

extra virgin olive oil, for drizzling

1 punnet shiso and basil sprouts, for garnishing
  (optional)

For the salad (optional)

2 baby artichokes

2 tablespoons lemon juice

1 tablespoons olive oil

a few sprigs of lamb's lettuce

shaved Parmesan cheese

salt and pepper

To make the ravioli, fill a large saucepan with water and add the juice of 1 lemon, the lemon halves, bay leaves, garlic, thyme and seasoning. Cut horizontally through the middle of each artichoke and discard the top half. Cut off the artichoke stalks and remove all leaves until just the hearts remain. Remove the chokes with a teaspoon and discard. Trim up each artichoke, remembering that whatever is green is tough and what's yellow is tender. As each artichoke heart is prepared, drop it into the pan of acidulated water to prevent it from discolouring. When both are in the water, cover with parchment paper and place a small plate or saucer on top to keep them submerged. Bring to the boil, then reduce the heat, simmering for about 15 minutes or until tender. Remove from the heat and leave to cool in the liquid. When cool, drain and finely dice the cooked hearts and set aside.

In a bowl, mash the goat's cheese until creamy, add the Parmesan, diced artichokes, pine nuts, reserved lemon zest and basil; season again with sea salt and black pepper.

To make the ravioli, place a heaped teaspoon of the artichoke mixture in the middle of each wonton skin. Fold the skin over to form a triangle and seal by brushing the corners with a little water, ensuring there are no air bubbles. Place on a baking tray dusted with flour and refrigerate until required.

To prepare the salad, remove the tough outer leaves from the artichokes, cut in half lengthways and remove the purple choke. Place the trimmed and cleaned artichokes in a bowl of water acidulated with half the lemon juice. Using a Japanese mandolin, shave the raw baby artichokes into paper-thin slices, place in a bowl and toss with the remaining lemon juice, olive oil, lamb's lettuce and Parmesan. Season with salt and pepper.

Cook the ravioli in a large pot of salted boiling water for about 2–3 minutes. Remove with a slotted spoon, drizzle with olive oil and serve with the shaved raw artichoke salad. Garnish with shiso and basil sprouts.

GRIDDLED RADICCHIO AND STRAWBERRY RISOTTO

Italians love their seasonal produce; so much so that they often have festivals to celebrate it. It was during *festa di fragole* (the strawberry festival) that I first tasted a risotto like this one. You are probably thinking that it sounds a little strange, but the bitterness of the radicchio really does work with the sweetness of the strawberries. It is best served with some reduced balsamic vinegar (see note below). serves 4

For the radicchio

1 head radicchio, approximately 350g

olive oil, for drizzling

sea salt

balsamic vinegar (approximately 2 tablespoons)

For the risotto

2 tablespoons olive oil

50g butter

4 shallots, finely diced

375g risotto rice (such as **Arborio** or **Carnaroli**)

300ml white wine

900ml hot vegetable stock

juice of half a lemon

4 tablespoons mascarpone

sea salt and pepper

50g Parmesan cheese, grated

8 strawberries, quartered

1 tablespoon finely chopped chives (optional)

Preheat a griddle pan over a medium heat. Cut the radicchio into quarters lengthways, keeping some of the stem attached to each quarter (trim off any dark parts of the stem). Open the leaves a little, drizzle with olive oil and season with salt. Place the oiled radicchio on the hot griddle and cook for 2–3 minutes on either side. When it begins to brown, remove to a plate and drizzle with a little balsamic vinegar. Leave to cool before shredding into thin strips.

To make the risotto, heat the olive oil and butter in a heavy-based saucepan over a medium heat, add the shallots and cook till translucent. Add the rice and fry for 1 minute, stirring to prevent it from sticking. Reduce the heat a little and add the wine. Allow the wine to be absorbed before adding a ladle of hot stock (that's approximately 200ml, depending on the size of your ladle). Stir and allow the rice to absorb the stock before adding the next 200ml. Continue to add stock in this way, stirring frequently, until it has all been absorbed and the rice is 'al dente' (with just a bite to it). This will take about 20 minutes. Stir through the lemon juice, radicchio, mascarpone and salt and pepper to taste. Turn off the heat, stir in the Parmesan and half the strawberries.

Serve, garnished with the remaining strawberries, chives, a drizzle of olive oil and reduced balsamic vinegar (below) or an aged balsamic (which is optional).

note Pour a bottle of balsamic vinegar into a small saucepan and warm over a low heat (don't use an expensive balsamic for this). Continue to heat until the balsamic has reduced and coats the back of a spoon. Turn off the heat and pour into a container. Leave to cool before covering; there is no need to refrigerate. If it thickens too much, gently warm in a microwave or in a bowl of boiling water for 5 seconds. This is great served over risotto, salads and fresh figs with honey. Cabernet Sauvignon vinegar is also delicious reduced.

BUTTERNUT SQUASH BARLEY RISOTTO

Traditionally, risotto is made with rice, but making it with barley gives it a wonderful nutty texture. One of the best things about this dish is the stock; there is so much flavour in the squash skins, and although most people discard them, they do make a marvellous stock. Whenever you use a squash, make a stock and store it in the freezer – it's so much tastier than a cube! serves 4

For the butternut squash stock

2 tablespoons of olive oil

I Spanish onion

I large butternut squash

I bay leaf

I cinnamon stick

I carrot

3 garlic cloves

For the risotto

I peeled butternut squash from above

50ml olive oil

salt and pepper

pinch of nutmeg

2 shallots, peeled and finely diced

I teaspoon ground cumin

400g pearl barley

100ml dry white wine

I litre hot squash stock (approximately)

juice and finely gated zest of I lemon

60g fresh Parmesan cheese, finely grated

2 tablespoons chopped mint leaves

40ml pumpkin seed oil (optional)

rocket salad, to serve

Make the stock: In a large pan, heat a dash of olive oil. Halve and slice the onion, leaving the skin on and cook over a high heat for 2 minutes. Peel the squash and add the peelings to the pot, along with the bay leaf, cinnamon, carrot and garlic. Continue to cook over a high heat for a further 2 minutes. Cut the top half from the squash and cut the bulbous part in half lengthways. Scoop out the seeds and add these to the stock. Add 2½ litres of water, bring to the boil, then reduce to a simmer and cook for 30 minutes. Strain and return to the pan, if using for risotto, straight away; otherwise leave to cool, then refrigerate or freeze.

Preheat the oven to 180°C/350°F/Gas Mark 4.

Cut the top half of the squash into 1cm dice and set aside; cut the bulbous half into rough 2cm chunks. Place the chunks of squash on a roasting tray, drizzle with olive oil, season with salt, pepper and a little grated nutmeg and roast until softened, about 20 minutes. Remove from the oven and purée until smooth.

Meanwhile, heat a dash of olive oil in a large pan and, once hot, add the shallots, cumin and diced squash. Cook over a medium heat until golden. Add the barley and cook for 1 minute, stirring constantly. Add the wine and allow the barley to absorb all the liquid. Repeat with a large ladleful of hot squash stock, making sure it is absorbed before adding the next. Cook until the barley is tender and most of the stock has been absorbed, about 30 minutes. Stir in the squash purée and warm through, then remove from the heat and add the lemon juice and zest to taste, Parmesan and mint. Check the seasoning and drizzle with pumpkin seed oil. Serve, topped with some rocket leaves.

POTATO GNOCCHI

The first time I ever made gnocchi it was a complete disaster! Having spent some time in Italy, however, I can safely say they are now much improved. My tips to you are, first, make sure you have enough surface area to make a floury mess, and second, don't be tempted to go overboard with the flour – you can always add, but you can't take away.

Serve it in the summer tossed with fresh peas, broad beans, a little ricotta and some torn mint. Or go for the classic version, as below, with a simple tomato sauce, basil and Parmesan. Use Sage Burnt Butter (see p. 160) as another alternative with some quartered, char-grilled artichokes from the deli counter and some Parmesan.

serves 4

1kg large, floury potatoes (such as King Edward, Marfona or Maris Piper)
150–200g plain or '00' flour, plus extra for dusting
salt and pepper
pinch of freshly grated nutmeg

1 egg, lightly beaten
Fresh Cherry Vine Tomato Sauce (see p. 156)
handful of fresh basil leaves, torn
freshly grated Parmesan cheese, to serve

Preheat the oven to 200°C/400°F/Gas Mark 6.

Place the potatoes on a non-stick baking tray and bake until soft in the middle when pierced, 1½–2 hours, depending on their size. Remove the potatoes from the oven and, when cool enough to handle, cut in half and scoop out the flesh using a spoon. Pass through a mouli or ricer (it is important that the potatoes are still warm at this stage).

Place the potatoes on a clean work surface, season well, sprinkle with nutmeg and two thirds of the flour and lightly knead together. Make a well in the centre, pour in the eggs and gradually work into the potato to form a soft dough, taking care not to overwork the mixture, and adding more flour if the mixture is too wet. (But be careful not to add too much flour, as the more flour added, the firmer the gnocchi will be.)

Before you progress, check the dough by cooking a few gnocchi to see how they taste and if they hold together. Taking approximately 1 teaspoon of the dough at a time, roll into balls and cook in a pan of boiling salted water for 2–3 minutes until they float. Remove and check for seasoning. Add a little more flour if they fall apart.

Cut the gnocchi mixture into quarters. On a lightly floured surface, roll each piece into a sausage shape approximately 2cm in diameter, then cut into 3cm pieces.

Place the gnocchi on a floured tray. (Traditionally, the shaped gnocchi pieces are rolled against the back of a fork to make gentle grooves; these help the sauce stick to the pasta, but in this case I don't think it matters.) At this point the gnocchi can be refrigerated for up to 5 hours, if desired.

To cook, drop batches of the gnocchi into a large pan of boiling water and cook for 2–3 minutes, or until they rise to the surface; using a slotted spoon, lift out and place in a warmed serving dish until all are cooked. Toss with fresh tomato sauce and basil leaves and scatter with freshly grated Parmesan.

QUINOA, MUSHROOM AND CHICKPEA CABBAGE ROLLS

I didn't like quinoa when I first tried it; I thought it was bland and boring! Then it became really trendy and was labelled as a 'super food' so I thought I'd experiment! Hopefully you will agree it's actually quite tasty with an interesting texture. Try varying this recipe by adding some nuts, or serve the quinoa as a dish on its own sprinkled with gruyère. Try substituting the cabbage with chard leaves. serves 4

10g dried cèpes

4 tablespoons olive oil

1 onion, finely chopped

2 sticks celery, finely chopped

2 carrots, finely chopped

3 garlic cloves, finely chopped

100g chestnut mushrooms, finely sliced

100g quinoa

200ml red wine

sea salt and freshly ground black pepper

80g cooked chickpeas

1 large cabbage, such as Savoy

2 x 400g tins tomatoes, crushed

1 teaspoon sugar

pinch of sea salt

100g grated gruyère

Preheat the oven to 180°C/350°F/Gas Mark 4.

Cover the cèpes with 200ml of boiling water and leave to soak. Meanwhile, heat half the oil in a medium-sized saucepan. Add half of the onion, celery, carrots and garlic and set the remaining aside. Cook over a medium heat until softened. Add the chestnut mushrooms and cook for a further 3 minutes.

Add the quinoa and cook for a minute, stirring all the time. Pour in the soaked cèpes and their liquid, add half the wine and season generously with salt and pepper. Bring to the boil, reduce the heat to a simmer, cover and cook for approximately 15–20 minutes until most of the liquid has been absorbed and the quinoa is tender. Once cooked, re-season as necessary and stir in the chickpeas.

Fill a large pan with water, add a pinch of salt and bring to the boil. Using a small knife, carefully remove the core from the cabbage, peel away 8–12 leaves and cook in the boiling water for 5 minutes or until softened. Drain and run under cold water to refresh, then drain again.

Remove the tough centre stalks from each leaf, and lay the leaves on a work surface, vein side down. Place approximately 2 heaped tablespoons of quinoa mix on one half of the leaf, and roll up, folding the sides in as you form a parcel. The size of the leaves will differ so fill and wrap accordingly. Place in a large ovenproof dish, seam side down.

Heat the remaining oil over a medium heat, add the remaining onion, celery, carrots and garlic and cook until softened. Add the remaining wine and tomatoes, sugar and salt and bring to the boil. Reduce the heat and simmer until reduced by half. Pour over the cabbage leaves, cover with foil and cook in the oven until tender, approximately 40 minutes.

Serve hot, sprinkled with gruyère cheese.

PARSNIP RISOTTO

I first made this risotto with I worked at Coast with Stephen Terry, a chef I greatly admire. The purée adds a real creaminess and body to the risotto, and the thyme pesto complements the sweetness of the parsnips.

Parsnip peelings and trim make a wonderful stock, perfect for this risotto, or winter soups. I know this recipe might look a little scary, so if you wanted to substitute a vegetable stock for the parsnip stock, that would be fine too. You can prepare the stock and purée in advance. *serves 4*

for the parsnip stock (makes 2 litres)
1 tablespoon olive oil
1 Spanish onion, finely sliced
peelings and trim from at least 6 parsnips
for the parsnip purée
50g butter
2 parsnips
1 garlic clove, finely sliced
300ml milk
pinch of sea salt and pepper
for the risotto
3 large parsnips
25g butter

2 tablespoons olive oil
4 shallots, finely diced
350g risotto rice (such as Arborio, Carnaroli or Vialone Nano)
juice of 1 lemon
4 tablespoons mascarpone
sea salt and black pepper
50g Parmesan cheese, grated
Thyme Pesto (see p. 162)

Heat the olive oil in a large pan over a high heat. Add the onion and cook until coloured and softened. Add the parsnip trim and 2 litres of water, bring to the boil, then reduce the heat and simmer for 30 minutes. Strain, cool, and refrigerate or freeze until required. Next, prepare the purée. Top, tail and peel the parsnips, then halve, quarter and remove the woody centres, reserving the trim for stock. Slice the parsnip quarters into 1cm pieces.

Heat the butter in a small pan, add the parsnips and cook over a medium heat until lightly coloured. Add the garlic, milk, salt and pepper and cook until the parsnips are softened, about 12 minutes.

Drain the parsnips, reserving any excess milk, and purée until smooth, adding a little reserved milk if necessary.

For the risotto, top, tail and peel the parsnips. Halve and quarter them and remove their woody centres (reserve these for stock). Cut into 1cm cubes. Heat the butter in a small frying pan, add the parsnips, season and cook over a medium heat until the parsnips are caramelised and softened. Set aside.

Heat the olive oil in a heavy-based saucepan over a medium heat. Add the shallots and cook until translucent. Add the rice and fry for a minute, stirring to prevent it from sticking. Reduce the heat a little and add a ladle of hot stock. Stir and allow the rice to absorb the stock before adding the next 200ml. Continue to add stock in this way, stirring frequently, until it has all been absorbed and the rice is 'al dente'. This will take about 20 minutes.

Stir through the parsnip purée and the caramelised parsnips. Add the lemon juice, mascarpone and salt and pepper to taste. Turn off the heat, stir in the Parmesan and serve, topped with Thyme Pesto.

GINGER BEER-BATTERED STUFFED TOFU WITH ASIAN MUSHY PEAS

A delicious vegetarian version of fish and chips with a twist! You can either steam or fry the tofu. serves 4

For the ginger beer batter

220g plain flour, plus extra for dusting

2 teaspoons salt

2 teaspoons baking powder

pinch of cayenne pepper or paprika

450ml ginger beer or lager

2 teaspoons ground ginger or 4cm fresh ginger,
    peeled and finely grated

vegetable or corn oil, for frying

For the tofu

2 tablespoons grapeseed or peanut oil

2 garlic cloves, finely chopped

2cm fresh ginger, peeled and finely grated

200g shiitakes, stalks removed and finely diced

1 green chilli, deseeded and finely diced

1 spring onion, finely sliced

1 tablespoon mirin (Japanese sweet rice wine)

2 tablespoons soy sauce

2 tablespoons chopped coriander, mint or basil

2 blocks of firm tofu

50g flour

vegetable oil, for frying

salt and pepper

1 lemon, cut into 4 wedges

For the Asian mushy peas

2 tablespoons olive oil

2 shallots, peeled and finely chopped

1 garlic clove, finely chopped

1 x 400g tin marrowfat peas

1 red chilli, deseeded and finely chopped

juice and zest of half a lemon

salt and pepper

half a bunch of mint, picked and finely chopped

Make the ginger beer batter. Mix the flour, salt, baking powder and cayenne or paprika together. Gradually whisk in the ginger beer and add the ginger. Chill in the fridge for 20 minutes or more before using.

Make the stuffing; heat the oil in a frying pan and sauté the garlic, ginger, shiitakes, chilli and spring onion to soften. Add the mirin and soy sauce and cook for 2 minutes more. Remove from the heat and stir in the herbs; leave to cool.

Cut the tofu in half vertically, then turn the tofu pieces on their sides and slit to make a small opening in the middle. (The slits should not be too deep or too close to the edge to avoid breaking the tofu.) Using a teaspoon, stuff the mushroom mixture carefully into the slits, until they are full. Chill in the fridge until required.

If steaming, place the stuffed tofu in a steam basket in a wok of boiling water, cover and steam for 5–7 minutes. If frying, preheat the oil to 180°C/350°F. Dust each tofu block in flour, then dip in the beer batter (slit side up) and carefully lower into the hot oil. Repeat with the remaining 3 blocks. If you are using a small pan, cook in 2 batches (adding all the tofu at once will lower the temperature of the oil and will result in a soggy batter). Cook for 2–3 minutes on each side or until the batter is golden, then remove carefully. Drain the tofu on kitchen paper and season with salt.

For the mushy peas, heat the olive oil in a small pan. Add the shallots and garlic and cook over a low heat until softened. Drain the marrowfat peas and add to the pan along with the chilli, lemon juice and zest and 1 tablespoon of water; gently heat through. Stir through the mint, season with salt and pepper and serve.

MISO-MARINATED KATAIFI-WRAPPED AUBERGINES

Miso is one of the best foods you can eat, being high in protein, vitamins, minerals and essential amino acids. My friend Lori first introduced me to miso-fermented bean curd. Being a vegetarian, she was conscious of her diet in terms of nutrition, but also felt that the vegetarian food offered in restaurants lacked imagination. Ever since this introduction, I've used it as a marinade but a little miso, water, fresh vegetables, soy sauce, chilli and ginger make an amazing healthy soup. It's quick and easy, and if you just add a few rice noodles you've got an instant dinner. I eat miso like this at least once a week. Greek kataifi can be bought from most Middle Eastern shops. serves 4

For the aubergine

1 medium aubergine, stem removed, cut into quarters lengthways

salt and pepper

9 tablespoons yellow or red miso

2 garlic cloves, grated

4cm fresh ginger, grated

3 tablespoons soy sauce

3 tablespoons mirin (sweet rice wine)

1½ tablespoons sesame oil

1 packet kataifi pastry (Greek/Turkish pastry dough in long, thin strands)

200g butter, melted

vegetable oil or grapeseed oil, for frying

For the salad

a handful of beansprouts

1 avocado, halved, peeled, stone removed and mashed into large chunks with a fork

¼ cucumber, peeled and thinly sliced

2 spring onions, thinly sliced diagonally

1 serving Ginger-Miso Dressing (see p. 152)

a bunch of watercress, picked

1 punnet shiso sprouts

1 punnet coriander sprouts

2 teaspoons sesame seeds, toasted

1 lemon, cut into 4 wedges

To prepare the aubergine, season with salt and pepper and steam for 6 minutes or until tender. Leave to cool.

Mix together the miso, garlic, ginger, soy sauce, mirin and sesame oil. Dip the cooled aubergine pieces into the miso mixture.

Spread the kataifi out on a work surface and loosen the strands to the length of the aubergine. Brush with melted butter and roll each aubergine piece in the dough. Heat the oil to 180°C/350°F and fry the aubergine in batches for 1 minute or until golden.

To make the salad, toss the beansprouts, avocado, cucumber and spring onions in the dressing.

To assemble, divide the watercress between 4 plates and top with the salad. Add the aubergine and sprinkle with the sprouts and sesame seeds. Serve with a wedge of lemon.

CHILLI AND ROSEMARY AUBERGINE PARCELS WITH SMOKEY MASH

Aubergines are incredibly versatile. They lend themselves to so many diverse flavours and cooking styles whether they are fried, smoked, steamed, roasted, grilled, mashed or pickled. serves 4

For the aubergine and mozzarella parcels

2 large aubergines

6 tablespoons olive oil

sea salt and pepper

2 garlic cloves, crushed with 1 teaspoon sea salt

3 sprigs of rosemary

2 teaspoons fennel seeds, lightly toasted

2 red chillies, deseeded and finely chopped

500g buffalo mozzarella

For the smoky aubergine mash

2 medium aubergines

900g potatoes (such as Desirée or Maris Piper)

100g butter, diced

100ml hot double cream or milk

sea salt and black pepper

20 caper berries (optional)

To make the parcels, slice the aubergine lengthways into ½–1cm slices (you need 8 slices in all), lightly brush both sides with a little olive oil and season with salt and pepper. Heat a griddle pan (or barbecue, weather permitting) over a medium heat and cook the aubergine in batches until golden and tender (about 2 minutes on each side). Transfer to a shallow dish.

Strip the leaves from the rosemary and finely chop, then add to the crushed garlic in the mortar and pestle, along with the fennel seeds and chillies and crush. Add the remaining olive oil and mix well. Pour the marinade over the aubergines and mix through. Leave to marinate for 30 minutes or overnight in the fridge.

Remove the aubergines from the marinade and lay them flat on a work surface. (Reserve the marinade for serving.) Tear the mozzarella into 8 pieces and place one on the end of each aubergine. Roll up to enclose – and if you have some rosemary left, secure the parcels with a sprig, for a professional touch! Place on a baking tray and warm under a hot grill or oven until the cheese begins to melt.

To make the mash, prick the aubergines all over with a fork and char over a gas flame, griddle or barbecue, turning frequently, until blackened. If you have an electric cooker, roast the aubergine in a hot oven, although you won't achieve the same smoky flavour. Place the aubergines in a colander and leave to cool. Cut in half lengthways and, using a spoon, scoop out and finely chop the flesh and place in a colander to drain away any bitter juices. If you have a steamer, peel the potatoes and cut into 4cm pieces. Steam until cooked, about 30 minutes. Shake any excess water from the potatoes and place in a pan or flat-bottomed bowl. (If you don't own a steamer, place the potatoes in a large pan, cover with water, add a pinch of salt, bring to the boil and simmer until tender, about 25 minutes. Drain well and return the potatoes to the pan, place over a low heat and leave for a minute or so to remove any excess water. Turn off the heat.) Add the butter and, using a potato masher, mash until lump-free. Pour in the hot cream or milk and beat with a wooden spoon until soft and fluffy. Stir through the aubergine pulp, season with sea salt and pepper and serve.

Serve the aubergine parcels on the smoky mash, together with some rocket leaves, drizzled with the reserved marinade. Caper berries would be lovely with this dish too, as in the photograph.

SMOKY AUBERGINE, TOMATO AND CASHEW NUT CURRY

In 2004, I travelled around India for a month – a real trip for the senses, during which I tasted some amazing vegetarian food. I tried a similar curry in Rajasthan and couldn't wait to get home so I could have a go at my own interpretation of it.

If you don't have a gas cooker, try charring the aubergines on a barbecue or in a non-stick pan. The charring is what gives the aubergines their smoky flavour. I like this curry served cold with a green salad, pitta bread and Greek yogurt. serves 4

2 aubergines

2 tablespoons groundnut oil

1 small white onion, finely chopped

3cm fresh ginger, finely chopped

3 garlic cloves

2 fresh red chillies, deseeded and finely chopped

1 tablespoon garam masala

800g plum tomatoes (tinned)

1 teaspoon sugar

100g roasted cashew nuts, crushed

sea salt

1 lemon

a bunch of coriander, finely chopped

sprigs of coriander, to garnish

Preheat the oven to 190°C/375°F/Gas Mark 5.

Char one of the aubergines over a gas flame, turning frequently until blackened. Roast the other aubergine in the oven for about 15 minutes. Leave both to cool. Cut aubergines in half lengthways, hold on to the stalk and, using a spoon, scoop out the flesh. Place the flesh in a colander to drain it of any bitter juices.

To make the curry, heat the oil in a large frying pan over a medium heat. Add the onion and gently fry for 2 minutes. Add the ginger, garlic and chillies, followed by the garam masala. Cook for a further 2 minutes. Stir in the tomatoes, together with their juice, crushing them slightly. Add the aubergines, sugar and cashews; season with salt and simmer for 20 minutes. Finish by adding a squeeze of lemon juice to taste. You may need to add a dash of water if it looks a little dry.

Stir in the chopped coriander and serve, garnished with sprigs of coriander and an accompaniment of Coconut Basmati Rice (see p. 102) and poppadoms.

VEGETABLE PARCELS WITH COCONUT BRAISED RED LENTILS

This is a wonderful dish to serve at a dinner party. Each stage can be made in advance and all you need to do when your guests arrive is pop it in the oven.

Red lentils are a favourite pulse of mine. If you enjoy these lentils you could try adding extra coconut milk and serving them as a soup; whizzing a third of it in a blender would give it a bit more body. I always like to blanch red lentils (in most recipes you just go ahead and cook them), as I think blanching and refreshing eliminates any impurities. serves 4

For the lentils

50g tamarind pulp

130g red lentils

2 tablespoons vegetable or peanut oil

2 banana shallots, peeled and finely diced

1 red chilli, deseeded and finely diced

2cm fresh ginger, peeled and finely chopped or grated

2 garlic cloves, peeled and finely chopped

a small bunch of coriander (roots attached), finely chopped

2 stalks lemongrass, finely chopped

1 x 400ml tin coconut milk

juice of ½ lime

2 tablespoons soy sauce

2 tablespoons chopped mint

20 Thai basil leaves, shredded (optional)

salt and pepper

For the vegetables

8 asparagus spears, woody ends removed

2 bok choy, halved lengthways

8 baby corn

200g beansprouts

320g tofu, cut into 4 pieces

2 spring onions, finely sliced

Soak the tamarind in 150ml of hot water for 30 minutes. Place in a sieve over a bowl; and extract paste by rubbing soaked tamarinds through the sieve with the back of a spoon. Discard the skin and seeds and set the paste aside.

Meanwhile, put the lentils in a pan, cover with water, bring to the boil, then drain in a fine-holed colander. Rinse with cold water and leave to drain.

Preheat the oven to 180°C/350°F/Gas Mark 4. Heat the oil in a large pan, add the shallots, chilli, ginger, garlic, coriander roots and lemongrass and sauté over a medium heat for 5 minutes. Add the drained lentils, coconut milk, tamarind concentrate, lime juice and soy sauce and simmer, stirring occasionally, for about 30 minutes or until the lentils are tender. Leave to cool, then stir through the herbs and season with salt and pepper.

To make the vegetables, bring a large pan of salted water to the boil, add the asparagus and cook for 1 minute, then add the bok choy and sweetcorn and cook for a further minute. Add the beansprouts and cook for 30 seconds. Refresh immediately in cold water and drain.

To assemble, lay 4 squares (38cm) of parchment paper on a work surface. Divide the cooled lentils between the squares and top with the tofu and vegetables. Sprinkle with spring onions. Bring the 4 corners of each square of paper together and secure with a paper strip. Place on a baking tray and cook for 20 minutes. Serve hot.

SPICED SWISS CHARD WITH BUTTER BEANS AND COUSCOUS

Chard is often overlooked, but not only is it rich in iron and vitamins A and B, it is also two vegetables in one. Its leaves – stronger and more earthy than spinach – are great in risottos, tarts, soups and as 'wrappers' for parcels such as the Cabbage Rolls on p. 60; its stalks are great braised with a little lemon juice, white wine, olive oil and herbs. (If the stalks seem stringy, peel them like celery with a vegetable peeler.) This recipe uses both stalk and leaf, and because the stalks take longer to cook, they are added first. To vary the recipe, try using chickpeas instead of beans. Serve as a hearty dinner or use the chard as a side dish. serves 4

For the chard

a large bunch of Swiss chard

50ml olive oil

1 onion, finely diced

2 garlic cloves, finely chopped

4 teaspoons cumin seeds

2 teaspoons ground coriander

large pinch of saffron strands

4 teaspoons ground cumin

2 teaspoons sweet paprika

2 teaspoons smoked paprika

1 red chilli, deseeded and finely chopped

juice of 1 lemon

100ml vegetable stock

sea salt and pepper

1 x 400g tin butter or cannellini beans, drained

a small bunch of coriander, roughly chopped

a small bunch of mint, roughly chopped

For the couscous

350g instant couscous

80g golden raisins

50g butter, diced

350ml boiling water

30g pine nuts, toasted

8 tablepoons natural Greek yogurt, to serve

Slow-roasted Tomatoes (see p. 158)

Prepare the chard by cutting the stalks from the leaves, then wash it in several changes of water. Cut the stalks in half lengthways, then slice each into 4cm diagonals. Shred the leaves roughly and set aside.

Heat the olive oil in a large pan (with fitted lid). Add the onions and garlic and sauté until golden. Add the spices and chilli and cook over a medium heat for 5 minutes, until fragrant. Add the chard stalks, lemon juice, stock and seasoning. Reduce the heat, cover and cook for 10 minutes. Add the chard leaves and beans to the pan and stir. Cover and cook for a further 10 minutes. Remove from the heat, adjust seasoning and stir through the coriander and mint.

For the couscous, pre-soak the raisins in hot water for 10 minutes until plump, then drain. Place the couscous, raisins and butter in a bowl, add a pinch of salt and pour over boiling water. Cover with cling film and leave for 3–4 minutes to steam. Remove the film and 'fluff' with a fork to loosen the couscous grains, then stir through the pine nuts.

Serve warm with Slow-roasted Tomatoes (see p. 158), yogurt and a wedge of griddled bread. Also great with some Red Lentil Dhal (see p. 114).

TOMATO, FETA, ALMOND AND DATE BAKLAVA

Baklava is usually sweet, but I always like to think outside the box, and I find that once I do this, a whole new culinary world opens up before me. This recipe doesn't break any rules, but it certainly makes a wonderful-tasting dish, served hot or cold. serves 6

100ml olive oil

5 Spanish onions, halved and finely sliced

2 garlic cloves, peeled and finely chopped

2 teaspoons ground cinnamon

pinch of granulated sugar

a bunch of dill, finely chopped (or 3 teaspoons dried)

8 vine plum tomatoes, skinned and roughly chopped (reserve half of the juices)

3 teaspoons tomato purée

1 packet filo pastry (9 sheets)

150g melted butter

60g blanched almonds, whizzed to a crumble

100g Medjool dates, stoned and finely sliced

250g feta cheese, crumbled

6 tablespoons clear honey

Preheat the oven to 180°C/350°F/Gas Mark 4.

Heat the olive oil in a large-bottomed pan. Gently fry the onions over a low heat, add the garlic, cinnamon and sugar and increase the heat. Fry for about 6 minutes, until caramelised. Add the dill, tomatoes and half of their juices and the tomato purée and cook for a further 5 minutes, until reduced.

Unfold the pastry and cut in half; keep it covered with a damp cloth to prevent it from drying out. Brush a baking tray (approximately 30 x 20cm) with melted butter, line the tin with a sheet of filo, brush with butter and repeat until you have a 3-layer thickness.

Spread half the onion mixture over the pastry, top with half the almonds, the dates and half the feta. Sandwich 3 layers of filo together, brushing each with melted butter and place on top of the onion and feta mix. Top with the remaining onions, almonds and feta and again top with a 3-layer thickness of filo. Lightly score the top, cutting diamonds (see photo) or squares, brush with butter and splash with a little water. Place on a baking tray and cook for 30–35 minutes until golden.

Leave to cool a little before serving, then drizzle each portion with honey. Serve with Fennel Salad (see p. 100) or some tzatziki.

SOFA
suppers

DUKKAH-ROLLED SOFT-BOILED EGGS WITH CHICKPEA PURÉE

Dukkah is a fragrant mix of roasted nuts, sesame seeds and spices. serves 4

For the dukkah

50g hazelnuts, skinned

40g sesame seeds

5 teaspoons coriander seeds

4 teaspoons cumin seeds

2 teaspoons sea salt

½ teaspoon black pepper

½ teaspoon paprika

large pinch of cayenne pepper

For the chickpea purée

3 tablespoons olive oil

2 garlic cloves, finely chopped

pinch of cayenne pepper

½ teaspoon smoked paprika

1 x 400g tin cooked chickpeas, rinsed and drained

sea salt

For the wilted greens

1 fennel bulb

2 tablespoons of olive oil

1 garlic clove, finely chopped

500g mixed green leaves (such as spinach, rocket, dandelion, chard)

salt and pepper

juice of half a lemon

For the soft-boiled eggs

4 free range eggs, at room temperature

4 slices sourdough, to serve (optional)

To make the dukkah, heat the oven to 180°C/350°F/Gas Mark 4. Roast the hazelnuts and sesame seeds separately until golden. Then, roast the coriander and cumin seeds until fragrant for 2 minutes.

Transfer to a food-processor or large pestle and mortar, add the remaining dukkah ingredients and blend until a coarse mix is formed (don't overdo it, otherwise you will end up with a greasy mess). Store the dukkah in an airtight container until required.

To make the chickpea purée, heat the olive oil gently in a pan, then add the garlic off the heat and swirl to infuse. Add cayenne pepper, paprika and chickpeas and return to the heat. Add 150ml of water and warm through. Purée until smooth and season with sea salt. Keep warm.

To make the wilted greens, halve the fennel lengthways, remove the core and cut into wafer-thin slices. Heat the oil in a large frying pan, add the fennel and garlic, cook until tender, then set aside. Return the pan to the heat, add a dash more oil and the mixed leaves. Leave to wilt a little, then toss, return the fennel to the pan and add seasoning and lemon juice.

Next, boil the eggs. Bring a pot of water to the boil, then carefully lower the eggs in and cook for 5 minutes. Remove from the water, refresh under the cold running tap and leave to cool. Peel and set aside. (The eggs can be prepared in advance.)

To assemble, toast the sourdough slices (if using), warm the peeled boiled eggs in a pan of boiling water and remove with a slotted spoon. Drizzle with olive oil and roll in dukkah to coat. Top each sourdough slice with warm chickpea purée, wilted leaves and a dukkah-rolled egg. Serve immediately.

SUMAC-SPICED AUBERGINE 'SCHNITZEL' WITH TABBOULEH

Aubergines lend themselves to all manner of flavours and textures, and just to prove it, here they are 'shnitzeled' – coated and fried in a delicate mix of breadcrumbs, cheese and herbs.

Sumac is available at Middle Eastern food stores. It's a bright red spice ground from dried berries and it has a tangy lemon flavour. If you can't get hold of it, just double the lemon zest instead. serves 4

Puy Lentil and Feta Tabbouleh (see p. 100)

For the 'schnitzel'

1 large aubergine

100g fresh breadcrumbs

2 tablespoons ground sumac

15g Parmesan cheese, finely grated

10g mint, finely chopped

10g flat-leaf parsley, finely chopped

finely grated zest of half a lemon

sea salt and pepper

2 eggs

dash of milk

30g plain flour

olive oil, for frying

lemon wedges, for garnishing

First prepare the tabbouleh according to the instructions on p. 100.

To make the 'schnitzel', cut the aubergine into 2cm-thick slices. Combine the breadcrumbs, half the sumac, the Parmesan, mint, parsley, lemon zest and seasoning. Whisk the eggs with the dash of milk and place the flour in a bowl or plate. Dust the aubergine slices with flour, dip them in the egg mix, then coat with the breadcrumbs.

Heat the olive oil in a large non-stick frying pan and fry the aubergines slowly, in batches, for about 3–4 minutes or until golden brown on both sides. Remove with a slotted spoon and drain on kitchen paper. Season with a little salt, and sprinkle with the remaining sumac.

To assemble, place the tabbouleh on a serving plate and top with the warm aubergine 'schnitzel'. Serve garnished with lemon wedges.

MISO BROTH WITH RICE NOODLES

I make this dish at least once a week for dinner – it's a very satisfying meal and also makes you feel really cleansed! It's so quick and easy, too; you can even make it in the advert breaks, if you are having a TV dinner.

Mix it up with your favourite veggies; courgettes, sugar snaps, peas, all work, or try adding some tofu. My guilty pleasure is a splash of Thai sweet chilli sauce. serves 4

250g rice noodles

3cm fresh ginger, peeled and finely sliced

4 tablespoons yellow, red or white miso

4 spears asparagus, sliced into 3cm pieces

4 baby corn, halved

1 carrot, peeled and thinly sliced

100g brown cap mushrooms, thinly sliced

150g broccoli florets

4 tablespoons chopped coriander

50g beansprouts

2 spring onions, thinly sliced

1 tablespoons soy sauce

Cook the rice noodles according to the packet instructions.

Put 1 litre of water and the ginger in a large saucepan and bring to the boil. Reduce the heat and stir in the miso. Add the asparagus, baby corn, carrot, mushrooms and broccoli and simmer for 3 minutes. Add the coriander, beansprouts, spring onions and soy sauce. Cook for another minute.

Divde the noodles between 4 bowls and top with the vegetables and broth. Serve immediately.

THAI-STYLE ROOT VEGETABLE CASSEROLE

There's nothing better than coming home to a warm house and a hearty meal on a cold winter's night, and the earthy root vegetables with aromatic Thai flavours in this recipe provide a comforting meal.

For a creamier casserole, try substituting a tin of unsweetened coconut milk for 400ml of stock; just remember to heat it with the stock, as adding cold liquid to the casserole will lower its temperature and increase cooking time by ten minutes.

Try different root vegetable combinations, too. Celeriac, Jerusalem artichokes and butternut squash or even Brussels sprouts would all work well. serves 4

1 sweet potato

1 small swede

2 carrots

2 parsnips

2 turnips

3 tablespoons grapeseed or vegetable oil

1 onion, peeled and chopped

2 garlic cloves, peeled and finely chopped

2cm fresh ginger, peeled and finely chopped

1 red chilli, finely chopped

4 sticks lemongrass, finely chopped (optional)

600ml hot vegetable stock

3 tablespoons soy sauce

salt and pepper

a small bunch of coriander, finely chopped

Preheat the oven to 190°C/375°F/Gas Mark 5.

Peel and cut the sweet potato, swede, carrots, parsnips and turnips into 3cm cubes. Heat a dash of oil in a large frying pan over a high heat and add the sweet potato. Cook until coloured, then transfer to a flameproof, lidded casserole. Reheat the pan, adding a little more oil, and cook the onion, swede and carrots. Cook until golden, then add to the sweet potato.

Repeat with the parsnips and turnips and, once golden, stir in the garlic, ginger, chilli and lemongrass and cook for a further minute. Transfer to the casserole dish and pour in the hot vegetable stock and soy sauce. Place in the oven and cook for 20–30 minutes.

Remove from the oven, adjust the seasoning and stir in the coriander. Serve in deep bowls with a creamy mash or soft polenta.

note If you don't own a casserole dish, cook in a large covered pan on a low simmer for the same time or until the vegetables are tender. Also, if you're pushed for time, try pre-cooking the vegetables, then adding them to the casserole with the hot stock and continuing as above.

FRESH BORLOTTI BEAN CASSOULET

There are few things better than fresh borlotti beans – I actually get excited about them coming into season! They have stunningly beautiful mottled pink pods, with a flavour that's second to none; and they also have a great propensity to absorb flavours when cooked or marinated.

Serve these beans on toasted sourdough for posh baked beans on toast, a little shaved Parmesan and a few rocket leaves. Alternatively, add some shredded chard or cabbage for the last 15 minutes of cooking or serve cold as a salad with soft-boiled eggs and rocket leaves. serves 4

4 tablespoons olive oil

1 onion, finely diced

2 sticks celery, finely diced

2 carrots, finely diced

2 garlic cloves, finely diced

1 bay leaf

2 sprigs of oregano, leaves stripped and finely chopped

6 sage leaves

800g podded fresh borlotti beans

6 plum vine tomatoes, peeled and roughly chopped

salt and pepper

juice and finely grated zest of 1 lemon

a small bunch of basil, roughly chopped

Preheat the oven to 180°C/350°F/Gas Mark 4.

Heat the olive oil in a medium ovenproof saucepan or casserole. Add the onion, celery and carrots and cook until softened. Add the garlic, bay leaf, oregano, sage and beans and cook for 1 minute, then add the tomatoes and enough water to cover the beans by 3cm. Cover with a lid or foil and place in the oven, cook for 30 minutes or until the beans are tender, remove the lid and leave to cool. Adjust the seasoning and stir in the lemon juice and zest and basil.

Serve warm with crusty bread and aioli, or with creamy mash and sautéed greens.

note These beans are best made a day before eating, allowing the flavours to infuse.

BUTTERNUT SQUASH AND RICOTTA SAMOSAS

The samosas are delicious served cold – great for a picnic – or you could try making mini samosas next time you throw a cocktail party. For extra texture, add 4 tablespoons of toasted pine nuts to the ricotta mix. You can also vary the salad by adding some smashed walnuts, watercress or dates. makes *12 samosas, serves 4*

For the samosas

3 tablespoons olive oil

12 dried curry leaves

1½ teaspoons black mustard seeds

pinch of dried fenugreek seeds (optional)

1 onion, finely chopped

3 teaspoons cumin seeds

3 garlic cloves, finely chopped or grated

4cm fresh ginger, peeled and finely grated

pinch of chilli flakes or powder

3 teaspoons ground cinnamon

750g butternut squash, cut into 1cm dice

salt and pepper

375g ricotta cheese

12 sheets filo pastry (approximately 30 x 20cm)

75g butter, melted

Spiced Cherry Vine Tomato Sauce (see p. 156)

For the salad

1 fennel bulb, halved, cored and sliced wafer thin
(if you own a mandolin, use it!)

2 heads red chicory, halved and finely sliced

1 punnet shiso sprouts (optional)

a handful of rocket leaves

a little lemon juice and olive oil, for dressing

Preheat the oven 180°C/350°F/Gas Mark 4.

Heat half the olive oil in a large frying pan over a medium heat. Carefully add the curry leaves, mustard seeds and fenugreek seeds (if using) and cook until they start to pop. Immediately add the onion, cumin seeds, garlic, ginger, chilli and cinnamon and cook until the onion is softened. Transfer to a bowl and leave to cool. Meanwhile, heat the remaining oil and cook the squash over a medium heat until tender and season. Leave to cool, then add to the onion. Stir in the ricotta and adjust the seasoning to taste.

Lay out the filo sheets, keeping those you are not working with covered with a damp tea towel to prevent them from drying out. Place 1 sheet of filo on a work surface, brush with melted butter, place another sheet on top and cut into 3 even strips, lengthways. Brush again with butter.

Place a heaped tablespoon of the squash mix on the lower right-hand corner of each strip. Fold the top right-hand corner of the pastry over the mix to form a triangular shape, then flip the triangle over to encase and continue along the length of the filo until you reach the top. Seal the edges with butter.

Place on a non-stick baking tray and brush with butter. Repeat with remaining strips, continuing until you have 12 samosas. Cook for 20–25 minutes, until crisp and golden.

For the salad, put all the ingredients together (it might be difficult to find shiso sprouts, so you could try adding any other type of sprout or shoot such as alfalfa, radish, lentil or fenugreek) and dress with lemon juice and olive oil.

Serve the samosas with the Spiced Cherry Vine Tomato Sauce (see p. 156) and salad.

textures of beetroot As a kid I had only ever tasted pickled beetroot, turning me against it for some time. All I really liked about it was the colour! Then I went to Australia and New Zealand and discovered what I had been missing all this time.

Beetroot is such a versatile root vegetable; its sweet, earthy flavour and velvety smooth texture can be taken on such a culinary adventure. Here I've given the beetroot a Middle Eastern and Greek twist, creating a sensational-looking sofa supper. Don't forget, you can use the leaves – full of nutrition and taste!

BEETROOT KEFTEDES

Here are some beetroot fritters with a Greek influence. Serve hot or cold with Beetroot Tzatziki, salad and pilau.
serves 4

200g cooked beetroot, peeled and coarsely grated
2 spring onions, finely chopped (including greens)
40g grated Parmesan cheese
50g feta cheese, grated
1 egg, beaten
2 tablespoons finely chopped dill

2 tablespoons finely chopped mint or parsley
salt and pepper
75–90g breadcrumbs
75g plain flour
groundnut or vegetable oil, for frying
1 lemon

Mix the beetroot, spring onions, cheeses, egg and herbs together. Season, then mix in enough breadcrumbs to combine. Cover and refrigerate for 1 hour.

Shape the mixture into balls (golfball-sized), adding a little flour if the mixture is too wet. Season the flour and use to coat the balls. Heat the oil until hot but not smoking and fry in batches for 2–3 minutes until golden on all sides. Remove with a slotted spoon and drain on kitchen paper.

Serve hot with a squeeze of lemon and Beetroot Tzatziki (see p. 88).

BEETROOT TZATZIKI

Roast raw and scrubbed beetroot in foil in a hot oven until tender, or buy it already cooked (but not pickled). This is also great served with Red Lentil Dhal (see p. 114) and Cardamom Flatbread (see p. 116). serves 4

1 large or 2 small cooked beetroot, peeled
1–2 garlic cloves, finely grated or crushed
dash of red wine vinegar, preferably Cabernet
   Sauvignon

3 tablespoons finely chopped dill
dash of olive oil
250g Greek yogurt
sea salt

Coarsely grate the beetroot and mix with the garlic, vinegar, dill and olive oil. Add the yogurt and mix well; season with sea salt. Chill in the fridge for 30 minutes before serving to allow the flavours to infuse.

SPICED CARAMELISED ONION AND BEETROOT BULGAR PILAU

The earthiness and sweetness of beetroot blend perfectly with these spices and the bulgar and pine nuts add a unique texture. You could even try adapting it by sprinkling with pomegranates or a little pomegranate molasses. serves 4

3 raw beetroots
175g bulgar
3 tablespoons olive oil
3 onions, finely sliced
2 teaspoons cumin seeds
2 teaspoons ground cinnamon
1 garlic clove, finely chopped

pinch of chilli powder
400ml boiling water
sea salt
40g toasted pine nuts
3 tablespoons chopped mint
1 lemon

Preheat the oven to 190°C/375°F/Gas Mark 5.

Wash and scrub the beetroots, wrap in foil and roast until tender, about 30–50 minutes (depending on the size of the beetroot). Leave to cool, then peel and dice.

Tip the bulgar into a fine sieve and wash under cold water to remove excess starch.

Heat the olive oil in a large pan, add the onions and cook over a medium heat until caramelised, about 15 minutes, stirring frequently.

Add the cumin seeds, cinnamon, garlic and chilli powder and cook for a further minute. Add the diced beetroot, bulgar and boiling water, then cover and simmer for 15–20 minutes, until the water has been absorbed. Season with sea salt and stir through the pine nuts, mint and a squeeze of lemon. Serve hot or at room temperature.

GREEK BEETROOT SALAD

A perfect way to make use of beetroot leaves. Look for beets with crisp leafy tops. serves 4

3 medium-sized beetroots

2 garlic cloves

sea salt and pepper

2 tablespoons red wine vinegar, preferably
   Cabernet Sauvignon

6 tablespoons olive oil

2 tablespoons chopped fresh oregano (or
   2 teaspoons dried)

Remove the stems and leaves from the beetroot, wash and shake dry, being careful not to cut the skin of the beet or it will 'bleed' into the water. Wash and scrub the beetroot, leaving the roots intact, then boil in plenty of salted water for 30–45 minutes until tender. Rub away the skin, trim the ends and cut into chunky wedges.

Boil the stems and leaves in a separate pan of salted water for about 1 minute until tender. Drain and roughly chop. Crush the garlic cloves with a good pinch of sea salt, place in a large bowl and whisk with the vinegar, olive oil and oregano. Toss with the beetroot and leaves and season to taste. Refrigerate until required.

If making as a separate salad, try serving tossed with torn soft-boiled eggs, Chickpea Purée (see p. 76), toasted sourdough and sprinkled with dukkah (see p. 76).

CAPRI LEMON PASTA WITH PEAS, BROAD BEANS AND ASPARAGUS

While working aboard a luxury yacht as a private chef, I had the great fortune of meeting the skipper, Eric, who also happens to be a fanatic foodie. Whenever there was an opportunity, he would take the crew out to eat, and I remember one such dinner in particular, on a balmy summer's evening in Capri. In a beautiful courtyard restaurant we were served the most amazing lemon pasta; it quite simply took our breath away.

It is such a simple dish, yet perfectly balanced and bursting with flavour, and this is my interpretation of it, simplified to make a sofa supper within minutes. I've added vegetables, which you could vary (courgettes – green and yellow – would work as well as their flowers) or omit altogether.

If you only have dried pasta, just cook as directed on the packet, adding the vegetables 3 minutes before the end of cooking. serves 4

300ml double cream

juice and finely grated zest of 2 lemons

a bunch of asparagus

450g fresh broad beans, podded (or 160g frozen)

400g fresh pasta (such as linguine, tagliatelle or
    spaghetti)

450g fresh peas, podded (or 160g frozen)

4 tablespoons mascarpone

80g Parmesan cheese, grated

a small bunch of basil, torn

salt and black pepper

Put a large pot of salted water on to boil. Meanwhile, pour the cream and lemon zest into a saucepan and carefully bring to the boil, then simmer for 3 minutes.

While the cream is simmering, prepare the asparagus: Snap off the woody ends and cut into 3cm pieces. You could also peel the outer skin from the broad beans (that's what we do in the restaurant).

Cook the pasta, peas, broad beans and asparagus together in the boiling water for 3 minutes or until the pasta is al dente. Reserve 50ml of cooking water and drain the pasta, peas, beans and asparagus.

Pour the cream into the cooking pot, add the lemon juice, mascarpone and reserved cooking water. Return to the boil, add the pasta and vegetables, Parmesan, basil and seasoning and toss together. Divide between 4 bowls and serve immediately.

TOMATO AND COCONUT CURRY

A summery one-pot curry that's quick and easy to prepare. Allison, my flatmate, grows pots of tumbling cherry vine tomatoes in the summer, which means that I am always creating new tomato recipes in which to use them. Try varying the curry by adding broad beans, fresh peas or courgettes, or play around with the tomatoes, using a mix of green, tiger and yellow. serves 4

I tablespoon grapeseed or vegetable oil

I teaspoon black or yellow mustard seeds

½ teaspoon cumin seeds

10 curry leaves

3 garlic cloves, finely chopped or grated

5cm fresh ginger, peeled and finely grated

2 green chillies, deseeded and finely chopped

I small onion, finely chopped

pinch of turmeric

pinch of ground coriander

4 cardamom pods

4 cloves (optional)

I x 400g tin coconut milk

20g palm sugar, grated

3 teaspoons dried fenugreek leaves

800g fresh tomatoes, coarsely chopped

2 tablespoons fresh coriander, chopped

I tablespoon Thai basil, chopped (optional)

salt and pepper

Heat the oil in a large saucepan or wok, add the mustard and cumin seeds and let them pop for 1 minute. Remove the pan from the heat and add the curry leaves, garlic, ginger and chillies. Return to the heat and cook for a few seconds, taking care not to burn the garlic, then add the onion and cook until softened.

Add the turmeric, coriander, cardamom and cloves and cook for a further minute. Add the coconut milk, palm sugar and fenugreek leaves and simmer for 4 minutes. Add the tomatoes and simmer for a further 5 minutes, adding a little water if too thick. Stir in the herbs, season and then serve with rice or lentils and poppadoms.

CHERMOULA-MARINATED PANEER WITH AVOCADO FATTOUSH

Chermoula is a Moroccan coriander sauce. Fragrant, with a hint of spice and a zingy finish, it is absolutely delicious – fabulous with roasted carrots or with a chilled carrot soup and great with cherry tomatoes, green beans or aubergines. If paneer is not your thing, simply substitute it with halloumi or tofu.

Fattoush is a popular Lebanese bread salad. Don't be put off by the length of the ingredients list, as it is really easy to prepare and the end product is delicious. Traditionally, purslane is used – a pale green herb rich in omega-3s and with a unique mild, peppery flavour – but since it can be difficult to source, I have used rocket leaves here. *serves 4*

Chermoula (see p. 159)

For the paneer

225g paneer

2 tablespoons olive oil

For the avocado fattoush

2 pitta breads

2 tablespoons olive oil

½ cos lettuce, shredded into 1cm ribbons

a handful of rocket leaves, roughly chopped

4 spring onions, finely sliced

100g cucumber, cut lengthways and sliced into half moons

2 tomatoes, cut into 1cm cubes

4 radishes, finely sliced (optional)

50g flat-leaf parsley, leaves picked, left whole

50g mint leaves, coarsely chopped

2 avocados, roughly diced into 2cm pieces

1 tablespoon sumac

salt

For the vinaigrette

1 garlic clove, finely chopped

sea salt

2 tablespoons lemon juice

3 tablespoons olive oil

Prepare the chermoula in advance.

To make the paneer, cut it into bite-sized pieces and mix with the chermoula. Leave it to marinate for at least 1 hour (or overnight if you have the time); drain, reserving the chermoula. Heat the oil in a non-stick pan, add the paneer and cook over a medium heat until golden. Drizzle over the reserved chermoula.

To prepare the avocado fattoush, open up the pitta bread and toast on both sides until crisp. Leave to cool. Break the bread into small pieces and toss in olive oil, coating on all sides (this will keep it crunchy for longer). Combine the remaining ingredients in a salad bowl and season with salt.

To make the vinaigrette, crush the garlic with a pinch of sea salt and mix in a bowl with the lemon juice and olive oil. Chill in the fridge until required.

To assemble, dress the fattoush with vinaigrette, toss with the bread and serve immediately, together with the marinated paneer.

HALLOUMI, RAITA, ENDIVE SALAD AND CRISPY POPPADOMS

Add an interesting twist to halloumi with this fruity spice paste. Paneer would also work well or, if you're a vegan, try using tofu (but make sure it's well drained). The raita is great served with grilled aubergines, too. serves 4

For the spiced halloumi

2 x 200g blocks halloumi cheese, each sliced
    into 4 pieces

I tablespoon olive oil

8 poppadoms, cooked

For the spice paste

4 tablespoons mango chutney

2cm fresh ginger, peeled and grated

a pinch each of ground turmeric, paprika,
    cumin, coriander

half a bunch of chopped coriander

sea salt and black pepper

For the raita

6 tablespoons Greek yogurt

6cm cucumber, peeled, deseeded and finely diced

I Granny Smith apple, peeled, cored and grated

2 tablespoons finely chopped red onion

2cm fresh ginger, peeled and grated

pinch each of ground cumin and garam masala

juice of I lime

2 tablespoons chopped coriander

sea salt

For the salad

2 heads Belgian endive (white chicory),
    thinly sliced

½ bulb fennel, finely sliced

4 Medjool dates, stoned and julienned (optional)

1½ tablespoons shredded mint and coriander

a bunch of watercress, picked

For the dressing

juice of I lemon

4 tablespoons olive oil

I tablespoon white wine vinegar, preferably
    Chardonnay

salt and pepper

Heat the oil in a non-stick pan and add the halloumi. Cook for I minute on either side.

Meanwhile, mix all of the spices for the paste together. Remove the pan from the heat, top the halloumi pieces with the spice mix and place under the grill. Cook for about 3 minutes to heat the halloumi through.

While the halloumi is cooking, mix together all of the ingredients for the raita and season to taste with sea salt. For the salad, mix all of the ingredients together and dress with lemon juice, olive oil and white wine vinegar. Season to taste.

To assemble, place I poppadom flat on each plate, top with salad, half the raita and 2 halloumi slices. Break the remaining poppadoms into 3 pieces each and stand upright in the remaining raita.

PARMESAN POLENTA WITH POACHED EGGS AND ROASTED FETA

The traditional way to cook polenta involves a lot of stirring and takes about 1 hour and, although it is well worth the effort, quick-cook polenta can produce a delicious meal in minutes.

I'm always surprised at the number of people who say they dislike polenta. Of course, it can be bland with no seasoning or butter, but with the addition of cheeses, herbs, mushrooms, sweetcorn, and so on, it can make a wonderful meal.

This recipe is quick and easy to prepare and can work equally well as a supper or light lunch. serves 4

200g feta cheese, cut into 2cm cubes

olive oil, for drizzling

black pepper

pinch of chilli flakes (optional)

500ml milk

125g quick-cook polenta

60g butter

30g Parmesan cheese, grated

salt

Griddled Radicchio (see p. 110)

4 free-range eggs

Preheat the oven to 180°C/350°F/Gas Mark 4.

Place the feta on a large sheet of foil, drizzle with olive oil, season with freshly ground black pepper and sprinkle with chilli flakes (if using). Wrap the foil around the feta to form a loose parcel, place on a baking tray and roast for 8 minutes or until the feta is softened.

Meanwhile, heat the milk in a saucepan until almost boiling, reduce the heat and gradually whisk in the polenta and cook, stirring, until it thickens, about 5 minutes. Mix in the butter and Parmesan and season with salt and freshly ground pepper.

Meanwhile, prepare the Griddled Radicchio.

Now poach the eggs; see p. 150 for making Perfect Poached Eggs.

To assemble, divide the polenta between 4 serving plates, top with the roasted feta, Griddled Radicchio and a poached egg. Drizzle with olive oil and serve at once.

SMOKED PAPRIKA AUBERGINES WITH A MINT AND PARSLEY SALAD

These smoky spiced aubergines, dressed with creamy, garlicky tahini yogurt, make for a delicious salad or light lunch. I love to serve this rolled up in a warm flatbread; it's one of my all-time favourites.

You can easily vary this dish. Try cutting the aubergines into 1cm-thick rounds and adding some pomegranate seeds or a sprinkling of toasted nuts (such as pistachios) to the salad for a little texture.

Smoked paprika is available at all good delicatessens. Check the speciality aisle at the supermarket too – it comes in cute little tins! serves 4

For the marinated aubergines

2 garlic cloves

1 teaspoon sea salt

1 tablespoon smoked paprika

60ml olive oil

2 large purple aubergines (or 12 baby ones), cut in half

For the salad

15g flat-leaf parsley leaves

15g mint leaves

1 red onion, finely diced

400g cherry vine tomatoes, halved

a handful of rocket leaves

salt and pepper

To make the marinated aubergines, pound the garlic with the sea salt in a pestle and mortar, then add the paprika and olive oil.

Cut the aubergines in half lengthways, then cut each half into thick wedges. Carefully score each wedge with the point of a knife in a criss-cross fashion and rub all over with the marinade. Leave at room temperature for 20 minutes or overnight in the fridge. (Remove the aubergines 10 minutes before cooking if you refrigerate them, to bring them back up to temperature.)

Preheat a griddle pan or barbecue and cook the aubergines over a medium heat for about 10–15 minutes (turning regularly) until all the pieces are tender. If you are concerned about your kitchen smoking up, char the aubergines on the griddle then finish them in a preheated medium-hot oven.

Toss all the salad ingredients together, season, and serve with the aubergines, along with a large spoonful of Tahini-Yogurt Dressing (see p. 154), or wrapped in Cardamom Flatbreads (see p. 116).

STYLISH
sides

PUY LENTIL AND FETA TABBOULEH

I can't get enough of Lebanese cuisine with its fresh and enticing flavours.

It was Anissa Helou who first showed me the art of making tabbouleh. The secret of this beautiful dish lies in the way you chop your herbs – they should be lovingly sliced, very finely, to produce thin slivers with a minimum of bruising. The extra effort this involves really does pay off. Traditionally, tabbouleh is made with burghul wheat; here, however, I've replaced it with puy lentils, giving a different texture to the dish. Oh, and the feta's just me! serves 4

120g flat-leaf parsley, with stalks

50g mint leaves, picked

2 tomatoes, finely diced

1 small red onion, finely diced

150g puy lentils, cooked

½ teaspoon ground cinnamon

1 teaspoon ground allspice

salt

juice of 1 lemon

60ml olive oil

50g feta cheese, crumbled

Using a very sharp knife, slice the parsley as thinly as possible, starting at the leafy top and going all the way down to the stalks; repeat with the mint leaves.

Combine the tomatoes, onion, lentils, herbs and spices and season with salt. Dress with lemon juice and olive oil, stirring in the feta just before serving.

FENNEL SALAD

A deliciously textured and aromatic salad, great mixed with a few diced vine tomatoes and tossed through cold pasta. serves 4

60ml freshly squeezed lemon juice

120ml extra virgin olive oil

1 bulb of fennel

a bunch of watercress, picked

a handful of mint leaves

a handful of flat-leaf parsley, stalks discarded

100g Kalamata olives, pitted

1 punnet shiso sprouts (optional)

Whisk together the lemon juice and olive oil. Halve the fennel lengthways and remove the core. Using a sharp knife or mandolin, slice it horizontally as thinly as possible. Toss with the remaining ingredients.

COCONUT BASMATI RICE

To spice up your rice a little, you might like to try adding a stick of cinnamon while the rice is cooking, or some cardamom pods, star anise, lemongrass, lime leaves, lemon zest or chillies. serves 4

250g Basmati rice

300ml coconut milk

200ml water

pinch of salt

Wash the rice in cold water until the water runs clear; this will remove any excess starch.

Place the rice, coconut milk, water and salt in a large pan with a tight-fitting lid. (If you don't have a lid cover with clingfilm.)

Put the pan on a medium heat and bring to the boil, then turn the heat to low and cover the pan immediately. Cook for 12 minutes (do not be tempted to uncover the rice during this time).

Turn off the heat and leave the rice covered for a further 10 minutes, then fluff with a fork and serve.

COCONUT BRAISED POTATOES

When I dreamed up the idea for these potatoes one day, they turned out a treat; so much so that when my back was turned the chefs could not resist eating them. Ever since then I have always made extra to allow for the chefs' tasting portions. serves 4

I tablespoon vegetable or peanut oil

2 shallots, peeled and finely chopped

I garlic clove, finely chopped

I red chilli, deseeded and finely chopped

I½ cm fresh ginger, peeled and finely grated

30g bunch of coriander, roots attached

700ml unsweetened coconut milk

500g baby potatoes, halved lengthways

2 tablespoons Thai sweet chilli sauce

I tablespoon soya sauce

2 tablespoons Thai basil, chopped (optional)

Preheat the oven to 190°C/375°F/Gas Mark 5.

Heat the oil in a saucepan, then add the shallots, garlic, chilli and ginger and cook for 1 minute.

Remove the roots from the coriander and finely chop (if the coriander does not have roots, chop half the bunch). Add to the shallot mixture and cook until softened. Add the coconut milk, potatoes, sweet chilli and soya sauces and stir. Bring to the boil, then pour into a small roasting tin or ovenproof dish and cook in the oven for about 50 minutes or until the potatoes are tender.

Remove from the oven and stir in the remaining coriander (chopped) and the basil (if using). Check the seasoning, although you probably will not need salt as the soya will season the potatoes.

COCONUT BRAISED CHINESE CABBAGE LEAVES

These cabbages are delicious braised with coconut milk and infused with Asian aromas. Serve with jasmine rice and Tomato, Cardamom and Coconut Sauce (see p. 154) as a substantial main course, sprinkled with crispy shallots. Salt and Pepper Tofu would also complement and add extra protein. Alternatively, you could serve this as an interesting side dish. serves 4

I Chinese cabbage

3 tablespoons peanut or grapeseed oil

2 shallots, finely chopped

4cm fresh ginger, peeled and finely chopped

2 red chillies, deseeded and finely chopped

2 garlic cloves, finely chopped

roots from a small bunch of coriander, finely chopped; reserve leaves for a garnish

I x 400ml tin unsweetened coconut milk

3 tablespoons soy sauce

a small bunch of Thai basil (optional)

Preheat the oven to 190°C/375°F/Gas Mark 5.

Cut the cabbage lengthways into quarters. Heat half the oil in a large frying pan over a high heat. When hot carefully add the cabbage (stand back, as it will spit a little). Cook until coloured on both sides, then set aside. Heat the remaining oil and add the shallots, ginger, chillies, garlic and coriander roots. Cook until softened and translucent. Return the cabbage to the pan, add the coconut milk and soya sauce and bring to the boil.

Turn off the heat and cover the pan with foil (if your frying pan is not ovenproof transfer the contents to a baking tin). Place in the oven and cook for 15 minutes, then remove the foil and continue to cook for a further 5 minutes or until the cabbage is tender when pierced with a knife.

Garnish with finely chopped coriander and Thai basil leaves.

WATERMELON PANZANELLA

As you've probably realised by now, I am a big fan of watermelon! This is a sensational salad recipe and a great way to use up any leftover melon. As with all panzanella salads, it's important to let the flavours infuse before serving. Toasting the bread a little will help to keep it slightly crispier. serves 4

For the salad

10 slices ciabatta

2 tablespoons olive oil

1 small red onion, finely sliced

300g diced seedless watermelon

300g diced ripe plum tomatoes

125g diced cucumber

2 tablespoons capers, rinsed and drained

200g halloumi cheese, diced (or 100g halloumi and 100g crumbled feta cheese)

100g chopped Kalamata olives

a small bunch of basil, roughly chopped

salt and pepper

For the dressing

50ml red wine vinegar, preferably Cabernet Sauvignon

150ml extra virgin olive oil

1 garlic clove, crushed

pinch of sugar

sea salt and pepper

Preheat the oven to 200°C/400°F/Gas Mark 6.

To make the salad, tear the ciabatta into croûton-sized pieces, drizzle with olive oil, place in a roasting tin, and cook for about 5 minutes, until golden. Leave to cool.

Toss the remaining salad ingredients in a large bowl, add the ciabatta and mix together well. Season with salt and pepper.

To make the dressing, whisk all of the ingredients together and pour over salad. Allow the flavours to marinate for about 1 hour before serving.

BRAISED BROAD BEANS WITH LEMON AND DILL

This is a great way to cook broad beans when they are in season. Most of the work is in the preparation, but the end result is worth the effort. It's also one of those dishes that actually tastes better the next day.

Eat warm with Parmesan polenta chips, like the ones on p. 108 but without the rosemary, or at room temperature with buffalo mozzarella or shaved pecorino, pea shoots and toasted ciabatta for a light lunch. Or use the beans as a stuffing for globe artichokes (cook them in water with a little oil poured into the water, cover and simmer until tender) or beef tomatoes.

To vary the recipe, try adding some skinned and diced tomatoes when you cook the beans (you will probably need approximately 500g). Or if you're not keen on dill, try mint or parsley instead. serves 4

1kg fresh broad beans in their shells
    (approximately 375g shelled weight)
90ml extra virgin olive oil
1 white onion, finely chopped, or a bunch of spring
    onions, finely chopped
1 garlic clove, finely chopped
pinch of sugar

pinch of sea salt
300ml vegetable stock (can be Fresh Pea Stock;
    see p. 29) or water
juice of 1 lemon
a small bunch of dill, finely chopped
a handful of pea shoots, to garnish (optional)

Shell the beans, discard the pods and peel the outer skins, if preferred. Heat the oil in a large pan and gently fry the onion until softened. Add the garlic, sugar and sea salt and cook for a further 2 minutes. Add the beans and stock (or water) and simmer over a low heat for about 20 minutes, until the beans are tender and most of the liquid has evaporated. Remove from the heat, stir in the lemon juice and dill and adjust the seasoning as necessary.

Leave to marinate for 1 hour. Serve, scattered with pea shoots.

GORGEOUS POTATO MASH

Mash is a beautiful thing; it should be light, fluffy, creamy, buttery, smooth and comforting. Sandrine – one of my fabulous chefs – made the best mash I have ever tasted, and here is the recipe. It's naughty, but oh so very worth it! For a healthier version, substitute milk for the cream and olive oil for the butter.

Try and choose a floury potato (see ingredients, below); waxy potatoes are ok, but can be a little temperamental – you need to work quite quickly with them and they can sometimes be a little gluey. The other really important point for making a good mash is that the cream or milk should be hot; adding cold liquid to hot potatoes will result in a sticky grout-like mess, better for tiling than eating!

For a flavoured mash you could infuse the cream while it's warming with some strips of lemon zest, sprigs of rosemary or sage or 2 sliced garlic cloves, then strain before adding to the potatoes. serves 4

1kg potatoes (such as Desirée, King Edward or Maris Piper)
125g butter, diced

150ml hot double cream or milk
sea salt and pepper

For the steamer method, peel the potatoes and cut into 4cm evenly sized pieces and steam until cooked, about 30 minutes. Shake any excess water from the potatoes and place in a pan or flat-bottomed bowl. Add the butter and, using a potato masher, mash until lump-free. (Or you could pass the potatoes through a ricer or mouli if you own one, then add the butter.) Pour in the hot cream and beat with a wooden spoon until soft and fluffy. Season and serve.

If you don't own a steamer, place the potatoes in a large pan and cover with water. Add a pinch of salt, bring to the boil and simmer until tender, about 25 minutes. Remove from the heat and drain well before returning the potatoes to the pan and placing over a low heat; leave for 1 minute or so to dry out. Turn off the heat, add the butter and continue as above.

note Be careful with the seasoning if you are using salted butter.

ROSEMARY AND BUTTERNUT SQUASH POLENTA CHIPS

Quick and very easy to make, these are fantastic chips, best served with aïoli. Kids will love them!

Why not try substituting peas for the squash and basil or tarragon for the rosemary. Sweetcorn also works equally well (see p. 23). serves 4

250g quick-cook polenta

1.5 litres water

salt and freshly ground black pepper

200g butternut squash, finely diced

2 teaspoons chopped rosemary leaves

vegetable oil, for deep-frying

plain flour, for dusting

20g Parmesan cheese, finely grated

Bring the water and 3 tablespoons salt to the boil in a large saucepan. Add the butternut squash and rosemary. Reduce the heat to a gentle simmer. Slowly whisk in the polenta and cook for 3 minutes, stirring gently. Season generously with salt and freshly ground pepper.

Pour the polenta into a greased roasting tray about 1.5cm deep, then leave to cool before refrigerating until cold and firm (about 1 hour). Turn the polenta out onto a chopping board and cut into 24 chips, each approximately 8 x 2cm.

Preheat the vegetable oil in a deep-fat fryer to 180°C/350°F. Lightly dust the polenta chips with flour and deep-fry until golden, about 3 minutes. Remove the chips from the oil with a slotted spoon, shake off any excess oil and place in a large mixing bowl. Sprinkle at once with the grated Parmesan.

ROSEMARY POPCORN

A decadent popcorn, easily made by infusing olive oil with rosemary. Fabulous to serve at a drinks party. To vary the flavour, try adding a little chilli powder to the rosemary popcorn once cooked. Or infuse the oil with sage or finely grated lemon zest instead of rosemary. You could also pop the corn, then drizzle with truffle oil and sprinkle with sea salt.

Popcorn will never be the same again! serves 4

100ml extra virgin olive oil   **150g popping corn**

3 sprigs of rosemary   **sea salt**

Pour the oil into a small saucepan, strip the rosemary leaves off the sprigs and add the leaves to the oil. Warm over a low heat for 10 minutes, then set aside for 20 minutes or overnight to infuse.

Following the directions on the popping corn packet, make the popcorn.

When popped and still warm, drizzle with a little rosemary oil, sprinkle with sea salt, toss well to mix and serve.

GRIDDLED RADICCHIO

I guess radicchio is like Marmite; you either love it or hate it! My editor, Danielle, says her Italian grandmother used to cook it for her when she was a child and she hated it! I think radicchio is a thing of beauty. I love its colour and the way its white-veined leaves entwine. Griddling radicchio mellows its bitter peppery flavour and, splashed with balsamic, it's wonderful – even Danielle was converted. Try it with the Soft Polenta on p. 96 or in a Risotto (see p. 56); it's great shredded into salads with shaved Parmesan and pears – a classic combination. serves 4

1 head radicchio   **sea salt flakes**

olive oil, for drizzling

Preheat a griddle pan. Quarter the radicchio lengthways, removing any loose outer leaves.

Drizzle with olive oil, sprinkle with salt flakes and place on the hot griddle pan. Cook on both sides until wilted.

DINO'S GREEK PEAS

Thanks to my dad, Dino, I knew I wanted to be a chef at the age of just four. My parents owned a restaurant in Richmond, and I would eagerly wait for my mum to come and collect me from nursery every day, after which we would run back to the restaurant together and I would get to see my dad. He was always busy cooking and I found it fascinating to watch him. Sometimes, I was given jobs to do, like grating Parmesan through the cylinder grater, or feeding potatoes through the rumbler. I would be in my element!

Here is the recipe for Dino's peas, best made a day in advance so that the flavours can intensify overnight.
serves 4

2 tablespoons olive oil

1 small onion, finely diced

2 garlic cloves, finely chopped

2 teaspoons tomato purée

1 x 400g tin plum tomatoes, crushed by hand

1 teaspoon sugar

1 teaspoon ground cinnamon

200g peas

a small bunch of dill, finely chopped, or
    1½ tablespoons dried dill

Heat the olive oil in a saucepan, add the onion and cook over a medium heat until softened. Add the garlic and tomato purée and cook for a further minute. Add the tomatoes, sugar and cinnamon and cook for 5 minutes. Add the peas, 3 tablespoons of water, the dill and a pinch of salt and bring to the boil, then reduce the heat and simmer for 20–30 minutes, stirring occasionally.

Adjust the seasoning. Serve warm.

CARDAMOM FLATBREAD

Flatbreads are quick and easy to prepare; even more so if you are lucky enough to own a 'KitchenAid'. Experiment by replacing the cardamom with different spices such as chilli flakes, onion seeds or cumin seeds.

makes 8

¾ tablespoon active dried yeast
½ tablespoon sugar
250ml lukewarm water (test it with your little
   finger – if it is too hot it will kill the yeast and
   it won't ferment with the sugar)
400g plain flour

15 cardamom pods, crushed in a mortar
   and pestle
3 teaspoons sea salt
1 tablespoon extra virgin olive oil, plus extra
   for cooking

In a small bowl combine the yeast, sugar and water and leave in a warm place until foaming, about 10 minutes. Sift the flour into a mixing bowl and add the cardamom and salt. Add the oil to the yeast mix and pour into the flour. If you have an electric food-processor, use the dough hook attachment to form the dough; otherwise, roll your sleeves up and start mixing!

Once you have a cohesive dough, turn it out onto a lightly floured surface and knead until smooth and elastic, about 10 minutes. (Or, if you have a food-processor, leave it on slow speed while you have a cup of tea!) Place the dough in an oiled bowl, cover and leave in a warm place until doubled in size, about 1–1½ hours. Turn the dough out onto a lightly floured surface, knock it back and divide into 8 balls.

Using a rolling pin, roll out each ball into ½cm-thick pieces, arrange on a baking tray lined with paper. (You can make these a day in advance and leave them in the fridge until required at this stage.)

Preheat a griddle pan, brush each piece of dough with a little olive oil and carefully lay them oiled side down on the pan over a medium heat. Cook for about 1 minute or until golden and light bubbles rise from the surface, then turn and cook the other side. Keep warm while cooking the remaining flatbreads.

note If cooking in advance, reheat flatbreads before serving.

STUNNINGLY sweet

SOFT MERINGUE ROULADE WITH APRICOT AND MASCARPONE CREAM

This recipe is so versatile. Try substituting plums or strawberries for the apricots and use rose water in the cream instead of orange flower water. Other fantastic flavours include raspberries, mint, lychees and pine nuts. Or just make it simple and fill with whipped cream and lemon curd. serves 6

For the meringue

4 egg whites

190g caster sugar

1 teaspoon vanilla essence

1 teaspoon white vinegar

1 teaspoon cornflour, sifted

For the filling

6 apricots, stoned and quartered

25g caster sugar

2 pieces stem ginger, finely diced

500g mascarpone cheese

175g Greek yogurt

100g icing sugar

3 tablespoons orange flower water

25g pine nuts (optional)

6 mint leaves, shredded

To make the meringue, preheat the oven to 200°C/400°F/Gas Mark 6. Line a 23 x 33cm baking tray with parchment paper and lightly grease with oil.

In a bowl, whisk the egg whites until stiff. Gradually whisk in the caster sugar a little at a time and continue whisking until thick and glossy. Fold in the vanilla essence, vinegar and cornflour. Spread the meringue evenly into the prepared baking tray and bake for 10 minutes, then lower the temperature to 170°C/325°F/Gas Mark 3 and cook for a further 10 minutes.

Dust another sheet of parchment paper with icing sugar.

Remove the meringue from the oven and leave to cool for 2–3 minutes on the tray, before turning out onto the second piece of parchment paper.

Cool for a further 5 minutes, then gently peel off the first sheet of parchment paper from the top of the meringue. Roll up the meringue from the long side until ready for use.

To make the filling, heat a large frying pan, toss the apricots in the caster sugar and add to the pan with a splash of water. Cook for 3 minutes over a high heat until soft. Remove the apricots from the pan and leave to cool.

Put the ginger, mascarpone, yogurt, icing sugar and orange flower water in a bowl and whisk together until thick. Unroll the meringue, spread the mascarpone mix over the surface, top with the apricots, sprinkle with pine nuts and shredded mint leaves and roll up again, using the paper to help you. Refrigerate until required, then serve in slices, dusted with icing sugar.

note If apricots are out of season, use organic dried ones. Soak them in some hot water, then chop. Or, if you want to be really extravagant, soak them in warm Sauternes. Also note, the quality of rose and orange flower waters can vary considerably. Look out for the Cortas brand, which you'll find in Middle Eastern supermarkets – its flavour is so much more intense.

APPLE AND ALMOND BAKLAVA WITH TURKISH DELIGHT ICE CREAM

Of course, I had to include a baklava recipe in this section but, for me, traditional baklava is just too sweet. This recipe uses dried apple rings that are soaked, and although they are still drizzled with honey syrup it makes for a much lighter result. Use apricots or pears instead of the apples, if preferred. serves 4–6

For the baklava

100ml brandy

250g dried apple rings, roughly chopped

400g whole roasted almonds, roughly chopped

50g caster sugar

2 teaspoons ground cinnamon

8 sheets filo pastry

175g unsalted butter, melted

For the syrup

125g clear honey

250g caster sugar

150ml water

1 cinnamon stick

2 strips pared orange rind

30ml rose water

50ml brandy

For the ice cream

110ml double cream

110ml milk

30g skimmed milk powder

150g caster sugar

350g Greek yogurt

100g Turkish delight, finely chopped or diced

1 punnet blackberries

To make the baklava, preheat the oven to 180°C/350°F/Gas Mark 4. Brush the bottom of a 30 × 20cm baking tin with a little melted butter. Warm the brandy and pour over the apple rings. Leave to soak for 10 minutes.

Mix the almonds with the sugar and cinnamon.

Cut the filo pastry in half lengthways, then brush 1 layer with melted butter and top with another layer. Repeat 3 times and place in the prepared tin. Sprinkle a third of the almonds over the filo, followed by a third of the apples.

Brush another layer of filo with butter, and repeat as above, brushing each layer with butter. Place on top of the almonds and apples. Repeat the layers until the fruit and nuts have been used up, finishing with a layer of filo pastry. Do not brush the top layer with butter.

Using a sharp knife, score a diamond pattern in the surface of the pastry, no deeper than the top layer of filling. Sprinkle with a few drops of water to prevent the pastry from curling and bake for 20–25 minutes, or until golden. Remove the baklava from the oven and leave to cool.

Put all the syrup ingredients in a saucepan and bring to the boil. Simmer for 10 minutes, until the mixture begins to thicken and coats the back of a spoon; keep warm. Pour the hot syrup over the cooled baklava and set aside for several hours (or overnight), until the syrup has been fully absorbed.

To make the ice cream, whisk the cream, milk, milk powder and sugar together, then pour into a saucepan and bring to the boil. Remove from the heat and leave to cool. Whisk in the yogurt and churn in an ice-cream maker. After 5 minutes, add the Turkish delight and blackberries, continuing to churn until frozen. Transfer to the freezer until ready to use. Carefully lift the baklava diamonds out of the tin and serve with the ice cream.

BANANA BAKLAVA SPRING ROLL WITH GREEK YOGURT

I love bananas. My mum always used to make us banana and custard – lovely and thick – as a dessert when we were kids and occasionally, for a real treat, we might have vanilla ice cream with it, too. Sometimes, the simple things in life are best!

Try this recipe for brunch; it's delicious. serves 4

For the baklava

125g shelled walnuts

125g shelled almonds

1 teaspoon ground cinnamon

4 tablespoons caster sugar

4 sheets filo pastry

25g melted butter

4 bananas

1 egg, beaten

For the syrup

200g honey

200ml water

juice and zest of 1 orange

1 cinnamon stick

Greek yogurt, to serve

Preheat the oven to 180°C/350°F/Gas Mark 4.

Pulse the nuts, cinnamon and sugar in a food processor. Lay out 1 sheet of filo, brush with melted butter and fold in half vertically. Repeat with the remaining pastry to form 4 rectangles. Peel the bananas and place 1 in the centre of each filo rectangle, then top with equal amounts of the nuts.

Brush the sides of the pastry with butter and roll over the banana, then turn in the sides and continue to roll. Seal with butter.

Place on a baking sheet lined with parchment paper and cook for about 15–20 minutes or until golden. Remove from the oven and leave to cool slightly.

To make the syrup, place all the ingredients in a saucepan and bring to the boil. Simmer until thickened.

To assemble, slice the baklava, drizzle with lashings of syrup and serve with a large spoonful of Greek yogurt.

CHOCOLATE TRUFFLES

When I was head chef at Delfina's we used to give complimentary truffles with coffee and became quite famous for our unusual blends of flavours. People would often ask if they could buy them but, unfortunately, as they were so time consuming to make, we had to say no. Hopefully, a few of my customers will now be reading this book; this recipe is for all of you.

Once again, the credit for some of these combinations goes to my amazing chefs. Coming up with the most unusual and creative flavours became our unspoken challenge!

Here is the base recipe. makes 30

160ml double cream

200g dark chocolate (the higher the cocoa
   percentage the better), broken into small pieces

20g unsalted butter, diced

100g unsweetened cocoa, for dusting

Heat the cream and infuse with flavours (see below). Remove from the heat and cool for 30 minutes to infuse.

Reheat cream to almost boiling, then strain over the chocolate and butter, stirring until smooth. Pour into a plastic container, cool and then refrigerate until firm. Using a Parisienne scoop or melon baller, form truffles, drop into the cocoa powder to coat, then reshape by hand and refrigerate until required.

Flavour options

Orange and basil use the zest of 1 orange and any leftover basil stalks.

Lemon and thyme use the zest of 1 lemon and a few sprigs of thyme.

Lime leaf and chilli use 4 kaffir lime leaves and 1 split red chilli.

Cardamom and orange use the zest of 1 orange with a tablespoon of crushed cardamom pods.

Rosemary and sea salt use 3 sprigs of rosemary and then add sea salt (approximately 1 teaspoon) when mixing with chocolate and butter.

Cinnamon infuse the cream with 2 sticks of cinnamon, add 2 teaspoons of ground cinnamon to cocoa when dusting.

Pomegranate and mint decrease cream by 40ml, infuse remaining with any leftover mint stalks and add 40ml pomegranate molasses.

Lavender infuse cream with 3 tablespoons dried lavender.

You could also try experimenting with various liqueurs, but remember to omit about 50ml cream; otherwise the mixture will be too soft. Spices work well too – for example, try pepper, nutmeg, turmeric or ginger – and chopped, dried fruits and nuts add a great texture.

If you want to be really flash try dipping or drizzling the truffles in white chocolate.

BLUE CHEESE CHEESECAKE WITH STICKY FIGS

This is a baked cheesecake that works equally well as a dessert or cheese course. I've used a beautiful French cheese, Fourme au Sauternes – its subtle flavour and this cake are a match made in heaven. Alternatively, you could use Dolcelatte, or ask at your delicatessen for a subtle regional blue cheese.

Pedro Ximenez is a sensational sweet sherry that tastes like liquid toffee pudding. Once you've tasted it you'll always want to keep a bottle in your fridge – it's divine. Pour it over vanilla ice cream or serve it with a hot chocolate pudding. serves 8

For the cheesecake
250g digestive biscuits
90g unsalted butter, melted
240g cream cheese
4 large eggs, beaten
1 teaspoon vanilla essence
200g caster sugar

200g Fourme au Sauternes or Dolcelatte cheese, crumbled
For the figs
225g caster sugar
10 tablespoons sherry
6 figs, quartered

To make the cheesecake, preheat the oven to 180°C/350°F/Gas Mark 4.

Place the biscuits and melted butter in a food processor and blitz to form crumbs. Transfer the mixture to a 20cm springform tin and press it evenly around the base and halfway up the sides. Place the cream cheese in a mixing bowl and beat it using an electric whisk, slowly adding the eggs one by one, the vanilla essence and sugar. Fold in half the crumbled cheese.

Pour the cheese mixture into the crust and scatter the remaining cheese over the top. Bake for about 45 minutes, or until almost set. Leave to cool, then chill in the fridge for at least 3 hours.

For the figs, put the caster sugar and 6 tablespoons of water into a small saucepan over a low heat and simmer gently until the mixture turns into a dark caramel. Remove from the heat and gradually add the sherry, taking care as the caramel may spit. Return the pan to the heat and bring the mixture to the boil.

Remove from the heat again and add the quartered figs. Leave to cool, then refrigerate until required.

To assemble, place wedges of cheesecake on individual plates and serve with some of the sticky figs.

GINGER SORBET

A wonderful, zingy, palette-cleansing sorbet, perfect served with honeydew melon and some fresh basil leaves. Or you could add a scoop to a glass of champagne for a refreshing cocktail. serves 4

225g sugar

440ml water

juice and zest of 2 lemons

4 tablespoons finely grated fresh ginger

¼ honeydew melon, chopped, to serve

a handful of fresh basil leaves, to serve

Heat the sugar and water together and simmer for 5 minutes. Add the lemon juice and zest and the ginger. Pour the mixture into a container and leave to cool. Once cool, put in the freezer for about 3 hours, fluffing with a fork every hour.

BLOOD ORANGE AND ROSEMARY SORBET

The blood orange is such a beautiful member of the orange family – great in both sweet and savoury dishes. Here, it's teamed up with rosemary, which is a delicious combination. If you enjoy these flavours, here are some other ideas for experimenting with them: sweet rosemary pastry with blood orange curd, drizzled with chocolate; rosemary flatbreads topped with goat's cheese, blood oranges and some bitter leaves; rosemary halloumi or seitan skewers grilled with a blood orange, olive and winter leaf salad. serves 4

110g caster sugar

110ml water

large sprig of rosemary

220ml freshly squeezed blood orange juice

1 tablespoon Grand Marnier (optional)

pinch of salt

To make the sugar syrup base, combine the sugar, water and rosemary in a small saucepan and heat to a gentle simmer. Cook for 5 minutes, stirring until the sugar has dissolved. Remove from the heat and leave to cool and infuse, about 20 minutes. Strain the syrup and whisk in the orange juice, liqueur (if using) and salt.

Pour into an ice-cream machine and churn, or freeze and stir with a fork every hour until the mixture freezes solid.

FIVE-SPICED PLUM AND RED WINE SORBET

A great-coloured sorbet, and perfect for using up ripe plums. I've used five spice but star anise works equally well; I would also use orange rind in place of lemon. Try adding a scoop to a glass of chilled champagne! serves 4

500g ripe plums
170ml red wine
175g caster sugar
160ml water

2 teaspoons Chinese five spice
1 cinnamon stick
3 strips pared lemon zest (removed with a
        potato peeler)

Halve the plums, discard the stones and place in a saucepan with all the remaining ingredients. Cook over a medium heat, stirring occasionally, for 25 minutes or until the plums have broken down. Discard the cinnamon stick and lemon zest, purée until smooth, then pass through a sieve.

Leave to cool then refrigerate, covered, for at least 1 hour or overnight. Churn in an ice-cream maker, following the manufacturer's instructions.

PLUM CRÈME BRÛLÉE

Try serving this brûlée as part of a plum-themed dessert; for example, with Five-Spiced Plum and Red Wine Sorbet (above) and Cinnamon Spice Plum Cake (see p. 130). serves 6

3 purple plums
1 tablespoon caster sugar
1 vanilla pod
375ml double cream

3 egg yolks
60g caster sugar
3 tablespoons demerara sugar

Preheat the oven to 170°C/325°F/Gas Mark 3. Cut the plums in halve lengthways, stone, then toss with the sugar and sear, cut side down, in a hot frying pan. Cook until caramelised, turn over and cook for a further minute.

Split the vanilla pod along its length, scrape out the seeds and put the seeds and pod in a saucepan with the cream. Heat to just below the boiling point.

Meanwhile, whisk the egg yolks and sugar until thick and pale. Remove the vanilla pods from the saucepan and pour the hot cream over the egg mixture, whisking continuously.

Divide the plums between 6 ramekins and pour the brûlée mix over the top. Line a roasting tin with a tea towel and stand the ramekins in the tin. Pour hot water three quarters of the way up the sides, cover with foil and cook for about 30 minutes, until the brûlées are almost set. Remove the ramekins from the water and leave to cool. Refrigerate for about 3 hours. Just before serving, sprinkle the brûlées evenly with demerara sugar and blast under a grill for a few seconds, until the sugar is golden and caramelised.

CINNAMON SPICE PLUM CAKE

Another delicious way to use plums. *serves 8*

110g unsalted butter, softened

200g caster sugar

2 eggs

190g plain flour

1 teaspoon baking powder

pinch of salt

1 teaspoon grated lemon zest

1 tablespoon lemon juice

3 tablespoons milk

6 plums, halved and pitted

2 teaspoons ground cinnamon

Preheat the oven to 180°C/350°F/Gas Mark 4.

Grease and line a 20cm springform tin. Whisk the butter and all but 2 tablespoons of the sugar together until pale and fluffy. Beat the eggs and slowly whisk into the sugar and butter mixture. Once mixed, sift the flour, baking powder and salt into the bowl along with the lemon zest, juice and milk and fold through. Pour into the prepared tin.

Toss the plum halves in the remaining sugar, together with the cinnamon, then place gently, cut side down, on top of the cake mixture. Cook for about 50 minutes, until a skewer when inserted comes out clean. Leave to cool slightly before removing from the tin. Cut into wedges and serve warm.

textures of coffee

I so love a good coffee. I can't tell you just how fussy I am about the way my coffee is prepared!

This is a collection of recipes using coffee in different guises; it's amazing how adaptable it is. It can be used in savoury combinations – in coffee gnocchi or in red wine sauces, for example – but here it is on a sweet journey.

For a decadent dinner party dessert, try making all the coffee combinations and serve portions of each to your guests. It may seem a little daunting but all of these recipes can be made ahead of time.

CAFÉ LATTE ICE CREAM

serves 4–8

200ml milk
50g coffee beans
200g caster sugar

5 egg yolks
250ml double cream

Pour the milk, coffee beans and 50g of the sugar into a heatproof bowl and place over a saucepan of barely simmering water. Leave for 1 hour to infuse. (You could infuse the milk as above, cool and refrigerate overnight, then continue as below the next day.) Strain through a sieve into a clean saucepan and heat to almost boiling point.

Meanwhile, whisk the remaining sugar and egg yolks together until pale.

Pour the hot coffee milk over the eggs and whisk, then return to the pan and stir over a low heat until the mixture coats the back of a spoon. (Do not overheat it or the eggs will overcook.)

Pass through a fine sieve and whisk in the cream.

Leave to cool, then pour into an ice-cream maker and churn, or put in the freezer and stir every hour until it freezes solid.

COFFEE BEAN CRÈME CARAMEL

makes 7 baby ramekins (or 4 large ones)

For the caramel

110g caster sugar

20ml water

2 tablespoons strong coffee

For the custard

225ml double cream

1 tablespoon coffee beans

½ vanilla pod, split and beans scraped

1 egg yolk

1 egg

65g caster sugar

To make the caramel, heat the sugar and water over a low heat until the sugar dissolves. Increase the heat and bring to the boil without stirring; cook until golden. Remove pan from the heat and carefully pour in the coffee. Stir until smooth and simmer for 2 minutes, then divide evenly between the ramekins.

To make the custard, preheat the oven to 150°C/300°F/Gas Mark 2. Heat the cream, coffee beans, vanilla pod and beans over a low heat until beginning to boil. Remove from the heat and leave to infuse for 10 minutes. (Put the kettle onto boil now for your bain marie.) Whisk the egg yolk, egg and sugar until pale and thick. Strain the cream mixture into the eggs, whisk and pour into the ramekins. Line a small baking tin with a tea towel, place the ramekins on top and pour in boiling water to halfway up the sides. Cook for about 20–30 minutes for small ramekins and 30–40 minutes for bigger ones, until the custard is just set.

Remove the ramekins from the water and leave to cool before refrigerating for 2 hours or overnight. To serve, run a knife around the edge of each ramekin and turn the custard out.

Serve with Coffee Tuilles (see p. 137) and Coffee Poached Pears (see p. 136).

COFFEE POACHED PEARS

serves 4–6

750ml strong coffee

90g caster sugar

6 cardamom pods

2 cinnamon sticks

2 bay leaves

2 cloves

4 pears

Place the coffee, sugar, cardamom pods, cinnamon sticks, bay leaves and cloves in a small saucepan and bring to a gentle boil, heating until the sugar dissolves.

Peel the pears using a vegetable peeler, leaving the stalks intact. (For beautiful smooth edges, gently rub each pear in a clean tea towel. Thank you, Dave, for this hot tip!)

Place the pears in the coffee, cover with a circle of parchment paper and weigh down with a plate. Simmer for about 20 minutes, until the pears are tender. Remove the pan from the heat, leave the pears to cool in the liquid, then refrigerate. Strain the coffee mix and measure 300ml for the jelly (below) and set aside.

Reduce the remaining cooking liquor over a medium heat until syrup-like, cool and serve with cold pears, whipped cream and Coffee Jelly.

COFFEE JELLY

serves 4–8

300ml coffee poaching liquor (from poached pears, above)

2g agar agar

Heat the coffee liquor over a medium heat and bring to the boil, whisking in the agar agar. Reduce the heat and continue whisking, simmering for 2 minutes. Pour into a shallow container, leave to cool, then refrigerate until set.

Cut into cubes and serve with pears. (Alternatively, pour the mixture into glasses, top up with café latte ice cream or whipped cream, cool and refrigerate.)

COFFEE TUILLES

Tuilles are usually circular and curved in the centre, involving a rolling pin and lots of work. Here, I've suggested spreading the mixture out, cooking, then breaking into long shards. I think they look much more dramatic this way and are a lot less fiddly. serves 4–6

40g unsalted butter
2 teaspoons instant coffee granules
40g plain flour

40g icing sugar
1 egg white

Preheat the oven to 180°C/350°F/Gas Mark 4.

Gently heat the butter until just melted, add the coffee and stir to dissolve.

Sift the flour and icing sugar together and, with a wooden spoon, beat in the egg white and the butter mixture to form a smooth paste. Chill in the fridge for at least 20 minutes or overnight before using.

Spread the mixture thinly on a non-stick tray or Teflon mat and cook for about 4–5 minutes until beginning to brown at the edges.

Remove from the oven and leave to cool, before breaking into long shards. Keep in an airtight container if not using straight away.

ORANGE, LAVENDER AND ALMOND SYRUP CAKE

I don't think you can ever beat a syrup cake. This one oozes flavour, is wonderfully moist and has a beautiful texture. It's based on Greek walnut cake and Middle Eastern orange cake, but I've jazzed it up with the addition of lavender. (You can leave the lavender out, though, if it doesn't appeal.)

Try serving with an orange and basil salad and Ginger Sorbet (see p. 127) for a crowd-pleasing dinner party dessert. makes *1 x 20cm cake*

For the cake

250g butter

200g caster sugar

4 eggs

50g plain flour

2 teaspoons baking powder

juice and finely grated zest of 2 oranges

250g semolina

200g ground almonds

120g Greek yogurt

For the syrup

juice and zest of 4 oranges

8 teaspoons dried lavender

750ml water

2 cinnamon sticks

560g sugar

crème fraîche, to serve

To make the cake, preheat the oven to 170°C/325°F/Gas Mark 3. Grease and line the base of a 20cm springform cake tin.

Cream the butter and sugar until pale. Beat in the eggs, one at a time. Sift in the flour and baking powder, then fold through the orange zest, semolina and ground almonds. Add the orange juice and yogurt, and stir gently until combined.

Pour into the prepared tin and cook for about 1 hour or until firm to the touch and a skewer comes out clean when inserted into the centre.

Meanwhile, make the syrup: put all the ingredients in a pan over a low heat and slowly bring to the boil, stirring. Reduce the heat and simmer for 20 minutes or until syrupy.

Remove the cake from the oven and pierce all over with a skewer. Pour half the hot syrup over the warm cake and leave to cool.

To serve, drizzle the cake with the remaining syrup and a large spoonful of crème fraîche.

note You can use any leftover syrup on the honey dough pastries on p. 147.

LEMON, ALMOND AND WHITE CHOCOLATE BROWNIE

A delicious brownie recipe. The lemon and almonds complement the white chocolate beautifully. The quality of white chocolate can vary tremendously so be sure to buy a good-quality chocolate. You might have to pay a bit more for this.

Try varying the recipe by adding some fresh basil leaves or thyme. If lemon doesn't rock your world, try it with orange and lime.

The secret to a great brownie is to not overcook it. You want to achieve a fantastically moist fudge-like density. makes *a tray or 10 squares*

200g dark chocolate, broken into small pieces

175g unsalted butter, diced

finely grated zest of 2 lemons

3 eggs

1 egg yolk

150g caster sugar

25g unsweetened cocoa powder

40g plain flour

100g white chocolate chips

50g flaked almonds

Preheat the oven to 180°C/350°F/Gas Mark 4. Line a 23 x 23cm baking tin with parchment paper.

Place the chocolate, butter and lemon zest in a small heatproof bowl over a pan of barely simmering water and melt the chocolate slowly. (Do not allow the water to boil.) Whisk the eggs, yolk and sugar together until pale. Fold the chocolate into the egg mixture. Sift the cocoa powder and plain flour into the chocolate mixture and carefully fold through. (This will create some air pockets and make the brownies light.) Fold in the white chocolate chips and flaked almonds.

Pour into the prepared baking tin and cook for 25 minutes. Check with a fork – the brownies should come out sticky, but not raw; return to the oven for a further 5 minutes if necessary. Leave to cool in the tin, before turning out and cutting into squares.

LEMONGRASS, GINGER AND LIME LEAF CHOCOLATE TART

This is such a decadent tart, combining rich dark chocolate spiced up with fragrant lemongrass, lime leaves and ginger. The lychees, filled with white chocolate and chopped lime leaves, add an element of surprise. Raspberries filled with this mix are equally delicious. serves 6–8

For the tart

275g dark chocolate, broken into small pieces

275ml double cream

4 sticks lemongrass, very finely chopped

3 teaspoons ground ginger

3 kafir lime leaves, very finely chopped

juice of I lime

6 egg yolks

I precooked Sweet Pastry tart case (see p. 164)

For the lychees

250g white chocolate, broken into small pieces

2 kafir lime leaves, finely chopped

I small can lychees, drained

cocoa powder, for dusting

To make the tart, preheat the oven to 180°C/350°F/Gas Mark 4. Place the chocolate, cream, lemongrass, ginger, lime leaves and lime juice in a heatproof bowl and heat over a pan of barely simmering water until the chocolate has melted. Stir until the mixture is smooth. Remove the bowl from the heat and leave to cool.

Whisk the egg yolks into the chocolate mixture, one at a time. Pour the mixture into the prepared pastry case and cook for 5 minutes, or until just set and shiny. Leave to cool, then refrigerate until about I hour before you are ready to serve (this is best served at room temperature).

To prepare the lychees, place the white chocolate and lime leaves in a heatproof bowl and heat over a pan of barely simmering water until the chocolate has melted. Remove from the heat and leave to cool until slightly thickened or piping will be difficult .

Spoon the mixture into a small piping bag, and squeeze into the centre of each lychee. Refrigerate until the chocolate has set.

To assemble, dust the tart with cocoa powder and serve with the chocolate lychees.

STUFFED FIG PASTRIES WITH HONEY AND NUTS

I so look forward to the fig season! In this recipe I've made a baklava-style nut filling and stuffed it into the figs, which are then rolled in kataifi (available at Middle Eastern delicatessens). If you can't get hold of the kataifi though, why not try dipping them in a light tempura batter and deep-frying? Delicious served with vanilla ice-cream, too. serves 6

150g honey

250g sugar

180ml water

1 cinnamon stick

2 strips pared orange rind

50ml orange flower water

For the figs

110g walnuts, shelled

25g almonds

25g hazelnuts, skinned

pinch of ground cinnamon

6 large Greek figs

1 packet kataifi pastry (or filo pastry)

150g unsalted butter, melted

vegetable oil, for deep-frying

300ml Greek yogurt, to serve

Heat the honey, sugar, water, cinnamon, orange rind and flower water in a saucepan. Bring to the boil, then simmer until reduced to a syrup. Remove from the heat and leave to cool.

Place the nuts in a food processor and pulse to a coarse breadcrumb consistency. Transfer to a bowl, add a pinch of cinnamon and just enough syrup to bind together.

With a sharp knife, criss-cross the top of each fig, gently squeeze open and pour in the sticky nut mixture.

Separate a little of the kataifi and place flat on a work surface. Brush the pastry with melted butter and wrap around each fig until covered. Keep the rest covered with a damp cloth to stop it drying out. Chill the figs in the fridge until required.

Heat the vegetable oil to 180°C/350°F in a deep-fryer and fry the figs until golden, about 1–2 minutes. Remove with a slotted spoon and drain on absorbent paper. Drizzle with a generous spoonful of syrup and serve immediately with Greek yogurt.

CHRISTMAS PUDDING BRÛLÉE WITH CARAMELISED BLOOD ORANGES

Use leftover Christmas pudding or any fruit cake as a base for these fantastic brûlées any time of the year. The blood oranges are so aromatic and make a perfect accompaniment, but if they are not in season, any variety will do. You can also try the oranges with meringue and crème fraîche as a great dessert – quick and easy.

serves 6

For the brûlées

1 vanilla pod

375ml double cream

3 egg yolks

60g caster sugar

150g fruit cake, diced

4 tablespoons demerara sugar

For the oranges

3 blood oranges

100g demerara sugar

2 fresh bay leaves

3 cardamom pods, crushed

3 cloves

3 star anise

1 cinnamon stick

150ml red wine

To make the brûlées, preheat the oven to 170°C/325°F/Gas Mark 3.

Split the vanilla pods along their length, scrape out the seeds and put the seeds and pods in a saucepan with the milk. Heat to just below boiling point.

Meanwhile, whisk the egg yolks and sugar until thick and pale. Remove the vanilla pods and pour the hot cream over the egg mixture, whisking continuously.

Divide the diced fruit cake between 6 individual ramekins and pour the cream and egg mixture over the top. Line a roasting tin with a tea towel and stand the ramekins in the tin. Pour hot water three quarters of the way up the sides of the ramekins, cover with foil and cook for about 30 minutes, until almost set. Remove the ramekins from the tin and leave to cool. Refrigerate for about 3 hours.

Meanwhile, peel the oranges and cut the flesh into 1cm-thick slices.

Heat the sugar in a large frying pan, add the bay leaves and spices and cook for 3–4 minutes, until the sugar has dissolved and is a golden caramel colour. Toss in the orange slices and cook for 1 minute, stirring continuously. Add the wine and heat for a further minute. Remove the oranges with a slotted spoon and arrange in a dish. Bubble the wine mixture until thick and syrupy, then remove from the heat.

Leave to cool before spooning over the oranges. Chill in the fridge until ready to serve. Just before serving, sprinkle the brûlées evenly with demerara sugar and blast with a blowtorch or put under a hot grill for about 1 minute, until the sugar is golden and caramelised. Serve with the chilled blood oranges.

note The brûlée recipe works as a perfect base for any brûlée flavour you might want to experiment with; for instance, try replacing Christmas pud with fresh raspberries.

HONEY DOUGH WITH GREEK YOGURT MASCARPONE CREAM

This is a wonderful dessert based on a Greek recipe for honey dough; it's a bit like doughnuts, but a whole lot lighter. It's so versatile too. Try adding a little cinnamon and mix and match your fruits (depending on the season) – stoned cherries, rose water, mint and pine nuts are delicious, as are fresh figs, roasted apples and blackberries (substitute almonds for the pistachios). It's entirely up to you. You can prepare the dough up to 2 days in advance. *serves 4*

For the honey dough

3 egg yolks

1 egg

25g butter, melted and cooled

25g caster sugar

finely grated zest of 1 orange

1 teaspoon vanilla essence

¼ teaspoon bicarbonate of soda

½ teaspoon baking powder

150g plain flour

vegetable oil, for frying

For the honey and orange syrup

5 tablespoons honey

juice of 1 orange

For the Greek yogurt and mascarpone cream

250g mascarpone cheese

90g Greek yogurt

50g icing sugar

3 tablespoons rose water

To garnish

1 punnet of raspberries

a handful of mint leaves, shredded

30g pistachios, roughly chopped

To make the honey dough, whisk together the egg yolks, egg, sugar, orange zest and vanilla essence. Sift in the bicarbonate of soda, baking powder and a third of the flour. Mix until smooth. Sift the remaining flour into the mixture and fold through until you form a soft dough. Turn out onto a lightly floured surface and knead until smooth and elastic. Wrap in clingfilm and leave to rest in a cool place for ½ hour. Lightly flour a work surface and roll out to a 0.25cm thickness; cut into rough 10cm square shapes. Refrigerate, covered, until ready to use (they will keep for 2 days).

To cook the dough, preheat the vegetable oil to 180°C/350°F. Fry in batches for 1–2 minutes on either side or until golden. The squares will puff up beautifully. Remove with a slotted spoon and drain on absorbent paper.

To make the syrup, warm the honey and orange juice in a small saucepan over a low heat until it forms a syrup-like consistency. Leave to cool.

To make the Greek yogurt mascarpone cream, whisk together the cheese, yogurt, icing sugar and rose water until thick. Refrigerate, covered, until required.

To assemble the dessert, pile the cream on top of the honey dough and scatter with raspberries, mint and nuts. Drizzle with the honey and orange syrup.

note When buying rose water, try to purchase from a Middle Eastern store, where you are more likely to get a higher concentration; my favourite is the Cortas brand.

SIMPLE staples

PERFECT POACHED EGGS

To me, there is nothing more gorgeous than a soft poached egg on toast. And it's so simple and easy to prepare. I am often asked how I poach my eggs. For best results, the eggs should be as fresh as possible (this means they will have firmer whites) and they should be at room temperature, too. The rest is easy.

Try drizzling the egg with a little truffle oil, top with some shaved Parmesan and serve with braised borlotti beans for decadent beans on toast! serves 4

4 free-range eggs
dash of white or malt vinegar
salt and pepper

Fill a medium pan with water, add the vinegar and bring to the boil. (The vinegar will help to coagulate the egg – that is to set the protein in the egg white; don't add salt as this will break down the egg white.)

Carefully crack each egg into a coffee cup or saucer.

Once the water is boiling, stir it to create a gentle 'whirlpool' (this will help to achieve perfectly shaped eggs). Carefully slide the eggs into the water, one at a time, and adjust the heat to keep the water simmering gently. (If the water boils too vigorously, the eggs will separate into yolks and whites.) Cook for 3 minutes, then lift the eggs out with a slotted spoon. Season with salt and pepper before serving.

note If you want to prepare the eggs in advance, cook them for 2½ minutes, then remove and place in iced water so that they don't continue to cook. (This is how we prepare them in the restaurant; we usually trim any straggly edges at this stage too.) When the eggs are required, reheat them in boiling water for no longer than 1 minute.

WHITE BEAN TRUFFLE PURÉE

This is such a delicious purée, and it's quick and easy to make. Spread it on bruschetta and top with sautéed cepes, a few rocket leaves and a little shaved Parmesan for a snack or canapé. It's also great with thyme and garlic-roasted baby beets and goes well with grilled fresh figs and rocket salad.

The recipe calls for 4 tablespoons of truffle oil but this may vary, depending on the quality of the oil used, so just add enough to suit your taste. I sometimes like to add a dash of lemon juice, too. serves 4

2 tablespoons extra virgin olive oil

1 shallot, finely chopped

2 garlic cloves, finely chopped

6 sprigs of thyme, stalks discarded

1 x 300g tin cannellini beans

4 tablespoons truffle oil

salt and pepper

Heat the olive oil and cook the shallot, garlic and thyme leaves over a medium heat until softened. Drain and rinse the beans, add to the pan and warm through with 50ml of water. Transfer to a blender or food-processor and pulse, adding truffle oil to taste. Season with salt and pepper.

note Truffle oil does not like heat, so always add it after the ingredients have finished cooking – treat it with love! Also, bear in mind that truffle oil goes rancid quite quickly, so if you've had some open for a while, sniff it first to make sure it is still alright – you wouldn't want to ruin your beautiful purée.

RAISIN AND OREGANO DRESSING

Serve this dressing with Chilli-Roasted Feta and Watermelon (see p. 18), or you could try it with Carrot Pancakes (see p. 14). Also great with warm borlotti beans or as a dressing for the Fennel Salad (see p. 100) that accompanies the baklava on p. 72. makes *enough for 4*

40g raisins

1 garlic clove

pinch of sea salt

1 small shallot, finely chopped

4 tablespoons red wine vinegar, preferably
    Cabernet Sauvignon

3 teaspoons vegetarian Worcestershire sauce

zest and juice of quarter of an orange

3 dashes of Tabasco sauce

150ml olive oil

2 teaspoons finely chopped fresh oregano
    (or 1 teaspoon dried)

Soak the raisins in hot water for about 20 minutes until plump, then drain and finely chop. Crush the garlic with the salt (in a mortar and pestle, if you have one) and transfer to a bowl. Add the remaining ingredients, along with the raisins, and whisk together. Store in the fridge until required; the dressing will keep well for up to a month.

GINGER-MISO DRESSING

Miso and ginger are a match made in heaven. Use this versatile dressing on almost any salad; it's great with edamame beans too. Or try serving it with pan-fried shiitake mushrooms and Salt and Pepper Tofu (see p. 113). It keeps well in the refrigerator. makes *enough for 4*

3cm fresh ginger, grated

1 garlic clove, grated

50ml rice vinegar

1 tablespoon soya sauce

1 tablespoon caster sugar

50ml sesame oil

1 tablespoon miso paste

2 tablespoons water

Whisk all the ingredients together and refrigerate until required.

TOMATO, CARDAMOM AND COCONUT SAUCE

This is a fabulous sauce that's great served with braised pak choi, tofu and jasmine rice. It also works well with fried polenta and wok-fried Asian vegetables or it can be served cold with char-griddled baby gem, soft-boiled egg quarters and rice noodles as a summery salad. serves 4

2 tablespoons grapeseed or vegetable oil

1 white onion, finely chopped

2cm fresh ginger, peeled and finely chopped
    or grated

1 red chilli, deseeded and finely diced

2 garlic cloves, finely chopped or grated

1 teaspoon ground turmeric

8 cardamom pods, crushed, husks removed

500g plum vine tomatoes

5g palm sugar, finely grated (see p. 170)

pinch of garam masala

juice of half a lemon

200ml coconut milk

2 tablespoons chopped coriander

salt

Heat the oil in large pan, add the onion and sauté over a medium heat until softened. Add the ginger, garlic, chilli, turmeric and cardamom, reduce the heat and simmer for 5 minutes. Cut the tomatoes into a small dice and add to the onion mix. Add the palm sugar and continue to cook over a very low heat for 15 minutes.

Just before serving, stir in the garam masala, lemon juice, coconut milk and coriander. Season with salt, warm through and serve.

TAHINI–YOGURT DRESSING

This dressing is delicious as a dip for crudités, or with some sautéed mushrooms (just add a little more water to thin it out, toss with mushrooms and sesame seeds and serve with mixed leaves). Also great as a simple dip served with the Cardamom Flatbread (see p. 116) serves 4

2 garlic cloves

1 teaspoon sea salt

300ml Greek yogurt

120g tahini

juice of 2 lemons

1½ teaspoons ground cumin

Pound the garlic and salt in a mortar and pestle until smooth. Transfer to a bowl and mix with the yogurt, tahini, lemon juice and cumin. Add 30ml of water and whisk until smooth. Refrigerate until required.

SWEETCORN RELISH

Perfect with piping hot Lemongrass and Sweetcorn Soup (see p. 36). serves 4

I corn on the cob, leaves removed

5 tablespoons olive oil

salt and pepper

I red chilli, deseeded and finely chopped

10g chopped coriander

I stick lemongrass, finely chopped

Roll the sweetcorn in a little of the olive oil, season with salt and pepper and cook on a preheated griddle pan or barbecue until tender. When cool enough to handle, remove the corn kernels from the cob, place in a bowl and mix with the remaining ingredients. Adjust the seasoning to taste.

AUBERGINE RELISH

Perfect with the Red Braised Mushrooms (see p. 50), but also great tossed through pasta or even with mature cheddar cheese on toast. You can easily adapt this recipe by changing the coriander for mint or adding a little chopped chilli for some heat. Best served at room temperature. serves 4

I aubergine

100ml vegetable or grapeseed oil

I small Spanish onion, diced

2 cloves garlic, finely chopped

Icm fresh ginger, finely chopped or grated

I teaspoon tumeric

½ teaspoon ground coriander

I teaspoon ground cumin

2 tomatoes, peeled and roughly chopped

juice of I lemon

2 tablespoons finely chopped coriander

sea salt

Cut the aubergine in half lenthways, then cut into 0.5cm-thick semi-circles.

Heat the oil in a large pan. Fry the aubergines in batches until well browned. Drain on absorbant paper.

Using a little of the frying oil, cook the onion in a separate pan until softened. Add the garlic, ginger and spices and cook for 2 minutes. Add the aubergines, tomatoes, 90ml of water and cook over a low heat for 5 minutes or until the water has been absorbed. Turn off the heat and stir in the lemon juice and season with salt. Leave to cool and then add the coriander. Let the flavours infuse for about I hour. Best made the day before. This relish will keep well in the refrigerator.

SPICED CHERRY VINE TOMATO SAUCE

If you like a bit of spice, add a pinch of chilli flakes to the recipe below. Try using this sauce tossed with spaghetti, fresh chillies and coriander for an Asian slant on a spaghetti arrabiata. makes *enough for 4*

2 tablespoons olive oil

1 teaspoon yellow mustard seeds

½ teaspoon cumin seeds

10 curry leaves

2 garlic cloves, finely chopped

2cm fresh ginger, peeled and finely grated

450g cherry tomatoes, halved

pinch of sugar

1 tablespoon tomato purée

pinch of sea salt

Heat the olive oil in a wok or frying pan until hot. Add the mustard seeds, cumin seeds and curry leaves and cook until beginning to pop. Remove from the heat. Add the garlic and ginger, then cook over a low heat for 30 seconds. Add the tomatoes, sugar, tomato purée, salt and 2 tablespoons of water and simmer over a low heat for 10–15 minutes until the tomatoes are softened and the sauce has thickened.

FRESH CHERRY VINE TOMATO SAUCE

Perfect for any over-ripe cherry tomatoes at the end of the summer and really easy to make. This sauce is great with gnocchi. makes *enough for 4*

2 tablespoons olive oil

2 garlic cloves, finely chopped

350g cherry tomatoes, halved

sea salt

1 tablespoon tomato purée

dash of balsamic vinegar

pinch of sugar (optional)

Heat the olive oil in a frying pan, add the garlic and cook for 30 seconds only. Add the cherry tomatoes, sea salt and tomato purée and simmer over a low heat for 10–15 minutes, until the tomatoes are softened. Add the balsamic vinegar and a little sugar, if necessary.

SLOW-ROASTED TOMATOES

These tomatoes are great served as part of an antipasto dish with buffalo mozzarella and some fresh basil leaves. If you have some sumac, add a teaspoonful to the salt and sugar mix, or try replacing the oregano with some picked thyme. serves 4

4 plum tomatoes

I teaspoon sugar

I teaspoon sea salt

2 teaspoons picked oregano (optional)

I teaspoon black pepper

olive oil, for drizzling

Preheat the oven to 170°C/325°F/Gas Mark 3. Slice the tomatoes in half lengthways and lay cut side up on a baking tray. Place the sugar, salt, oregano and black pepper in a small bowl and mix. Sprinkle over the tomatoes and roast in the oven for 2 hours. The tomatoes will become caramelised and semi-dry. Remove from the oven, drizzle with a little olive oil and set aside. Serve at room temperature.

note If you prefer to use cherry vine tomatoes, sprinkle the salt and sugar mix over a baking tray, place the tomatoes on top and cook as above.

CHERMOULA

Anissa Helou taught me the delights of Moroccan cuisine; I met her while attending one of her cooking classes, and she has been a dear friend and inspiration ever since. serves 4

50g coriander, including stalks

2 garlic cloves

1 teaspoon ground cumin

½ teaspoon paprika

pinch of chilli powder

2 tablespoons freshly squeezed lemon juice

salt

3 tablespoons light olive oil

Roughly chop the coriander and garlic and place in a blender with the cumin, paprika, chilli and lemon juice. Add a large pinch of salt and whiz. Gradually add the olive oil, blending until smooth.

APPLE RAITA

Sandrine, one of my fabulous chefs at Delfina's, helped me design this cool and refreshing raita. I love it as a snack with poppadoms and dhal; in fact, it's perfect with anything spicy. serves 4

4 tablespoons Greek yogurt

3cm cucumber, peeled, deseeded and finely diced

½ Granny Smith, peeled, cored and grated

2 tablespoons red onion, finely chopped

1cm fresh ginger, peeled and grated

pinch of ground cumin

pinch of garam masala

juice of 1 lime

1 tablespoon chopped coriander

sea salt

Mix together all of the ingredients and season to taste with sea salt.

SAGE BURNT BUTTER

This butter is great added to potato mash or stirred through crushed new potatoes with corn kernels and crème fraîche. serves 4

150g unsalted butter

12 sage leaves

2 teaspoons lemon juice

Heat the butter in a small saucepan over a medium heat until it begins to foam and turn golden brown.

Turn off the heat and add the sage leaves (be careful, as they will splutter a little). Add the lemon juice and set aside until required.

THYME PESTO

A great variation on a traditional basil pesto; earthy and interesting, and a perfect accompaniment to Parsnip Risotto (see p. 61). Try mixing it through pasta or mashed potato, or vary the recipe by changing it to walnuts, chestnuts or macadamias. If you have a nut allergy, substitute these for sunflower or pumpkin seeds. You can change the Parmesan to pecorino for a sharper, saltier taste. serves 4–6 *(for pasta)*

a small bunch of thyme
half a small bunch of basil
50g Parmesan cheese, grated
50g pine nuts, toasted

2 garlic cloves, finely chopped
1 teaspoon sea salt
juice of half a lemon
75ml olive oil

Strip the leaves from the thyme and basil and place in a blender with the Parmesan, pine nuts, garlic, sea salt and lemon juice. Blend until roughly chopped.

With the motor running, slowly pour in the oil, adding enough oil to form a medium-thick pesto.

Store in the fridge, covering the surface area with a little oil, until required.

SWEET PASTRY

A delicious sweet pastry perfect for lining tart cases. For an interesting twist, experiment by adding a little grated lemon, lime or orange zest. makes *1 x 20cm diameter tart*

200g plain flour

70g caster sugar

100g chilled, unsalted butter, diced

2 egg yolks

2–3 tablepoons milk

Mix the flour and sugar together in a food-processor. Add the butter and pulse until incorporated and the mix resembles fine breadcrumbs. With the motor running, add the egg yolks and enough milk to form a soft dough, adding more if necessary. If making by hand, rub the butter into the flour, add the sugar and then bring it together with the egg yolks and milk. Remove the pastry and roll into a ball; wrap in clingfilm and chill in the fridge for 20–30 minutes.

Preheat the oven to 180°C/350°F/Gas Mark 4.

Roll the pastry out between 2 sheets of baking paper (or on a lightly floured surface) until it is large enough to fill the tart case with a slight overhang. Remove the top sheet of the paper and invert the pastry into the tin, then remove the remaining paper and lightly press the dough into the tin, paying special attention to the edges. Cut away any overhanging edges, then rest in the fridge or freezer for 15 minutes (this will prevent the pastry from shrinking during cooking).

Line the pastry shell with paper, fill with baking beans or rice, place on a baking tray and cook for 10 minutes. Carefully remove the paper and beans and return to the oven for a further 5 minutes or until the base is dry to touch. Leave to cool in the tin.

CINNAMON SPICE AND ALL THINGS NICE COOKIES

I had a young agency chef turn up at Delfina's one day, her name was Paula, and she was Amazing! She was unhappy in her full time work so I offered her a job immediately! Miss P, as she became affectionately known, made the most amazing cookies; this is a version of her chocolate chip recipe. Delicious with a coffee or try serving as a dessert with roasted apple wedges and a dollop of Greek yogurt. makes 30

250g butter, softened
80g caster sugar
½ tin condensed milk
1 teaspoon vanilla extract
360g plain flour

2 teaspoons baking powder
3 teaspoons ground cinnamon
125g dried apple rings, finely chopped

Preheat the oven to 180°C/350°F/Gas Mark 4.

Cream the butter and sugar together until pale and smooth, add the condensed milk and vanilla extract and mix until combined. Sift in the flour, baking powder and cinnamon and then add the dried apple and mix to form a dough. Roll into a cylinder, approximately 4cm in diameter (at this stage you can refrigerate the dough and use as and when required).

Slice the dough into round pieces 1cm-thick and place on a non-stick baking sheet, leaving a gap between each. Cook for 15–20 minutes until golden.

note Try varying the recipe by substituting the apple for mango and changing the cinnamon to ginger. Try soaking the apples in brandy and drizzling the cooled cookies with plain chocolate.

STOCKS

Stocks are the foundation for many recipes and, as such, should be made with love! When making a stock, 40–45 minutes is adequate to extract the flavour; cooking for longer will result in a bitter-tasting stock. It should also be strained as soon as it's done, otherwise the vegetables will continue to cook in the liquid, again resulting in a bitter flavour.

Remember that too much of a particular vegetable will dominate the flavour of the stock, so when making a stock for a specific dish, consider which vegetables will complement it.

Stalks from fresh herbs make great additions, as do some peelings.

BASIC VEGETABLE STOCK

Use as a base for soups and risottos. Stocks are really versatile – for a fuller flavour add some field mushrooms.
makes *approximately 1–2 litres*

3 carrots

2 sticks celery

2 onions

1 leek

1 garlic bulb

1 tablespoon olive oil

3 sprigs of thyme

2 bay leaves

parsley stalks (from a small bunch)

1 teaspoon black peppercorns

Clean and roughly chop the vegetables. Heat the oil in a large pan, add the vegetables and sauté over a meduim heat until browned. Add the remaining ingredients, cover with water and bring to the boil. Skim any scum from the surface. Reduce the heat to a simmer and cook for 40 minutes; the vegetables should be well cooked. Strain and discard the solids.

Cool before refrigerating or freezing.

ASIAN VEGETABLE STOCK

Use in curries or in any Asian-inspired dishes. Perfect as a base for poaching vegetables and rice noodles for a light soup. makes *approximately 2 litres*

1 tablespoon grapeseed or vegetable oil
3 onions, peeled and roughly chopped
2 carrots, peeled and roughly chopped
2 sticks celery, roughly chopped
2 garlic bulbs, halved horizontally
8cm fresh ginger, thinly sliced
6 sticks lemongrass, bruised
1 red chilli

a small handful of mushroom stalks
25g coriander roots (or the stems from a
    bunch), washed
1 teaspoon black peppercorns
1 star anise
2 tablespoons soya sauce

Heat the oil in a large pan and sauté the onions, carrots, celery, garlic and ginger over a medium-high heat for 10 minutes. Add the remaining ingredients, cover with cold water and bring to the boil. Reduce heat and simmer for 40 minutes. Strain and discard the solids. Cool before refrigerating or freezing.

note Any of the following ingredients could also be used to enhance the stock: orange zest, lime zest, tomatoes, soya sauce, tamarind, cinnamon sticks, cardamom pods or fennel trim. For a more concentrated stock, strain the stock, put it back in the pan and by boiling reduce it by one third.

WEIGHT (solids)

7g	¼oz
10g	½oz
20g	¾oz
25g	1oz
40g	1½oz
50g	2oz
60g	2½oz
75g	3oz
100g	3½oz
110g	4oz (¼lb)
125g	4½oz
150g	5½oz
175g	6oz
200g	7oz
225g	8oz (½lb)
250g	9oz
275g	10oz
300g	10½oz
310g	11oz
325g	11½oz
350g	12oz (¾lb)
375g	13oz
400g	14oz
425g	15oz
450g	1lb
500g (½kg)	18oz
600g	1¼lb
700g	1½lb
750g	1lb 10oz
900g	2lb
1kg	2¼lb
1.1kg	2½lb
1.2kg	2lb 12oz
1.3kg	3lb
1.5kg	3lb 5oz
1.6kg	3½lb
1.8kg	4lb
2kg	4lb 8oz
2.25kg	5lb
2.5kg	5lb 8oz
3kg	6lb 8oz

VOLUME (liquids)

5ml	1 teaspoon
10ml	1 dessertspoon
15ml	1 tablespoon or ½fl oz
30ml	1fl oz
40ml	1½fl oz
50ml	2fl oz
60ml	2½fl oz
75ml	3fl oz
100ml	3½fl oz
125ml	4fl oz
150ml	5fl oz (¼ pint)
160ml	5½fl oz
175ml	6fl oz
200ml	7fl oz
225ml	8fl oz
250ml (0.25 litre)	9fl oz
300ml	10fl oz (½ pint)
325ml	11fl oz
350ml	12fl oz
370ml	13fl oz
400ml	14fl oz
425ml	15fl oz (¾ pint)
450ml	16fl oz
500ml (0.5 litre)	18fl oz
550ml	19fl oz
600ml	20fl oz (1 pint)
700ml	1¼ pints
850ml	1½ pints
1 litre	1¾ pints
1.2 litres	2 pints
1.5 litres	2½ pints
1.8 litres	3 pints
2 litres	3½ pints

LENGTH

5mm	¼in
1cm	½in
2cm	¾in
2.5cm	1in
3cm	1¼in
4cm	1½in
5cm	2in
7.5cm	3in
10cm	4in
15cm	6in
18cm	7in
20cm	8in
24cm	10in
28cm	11in
30cm	12in

OVEN TEMPERATURES

Celsius*/Fahrenheit	Gas/Description
110°C/225°F	mark¼/cool
130°C/250°F	mark½/cool
140°C/275°F	mark 1/very low
150°C/300°F	mark 2/very low
170°C/325°F	mark 3/low
180°C/350°F	mark 4/moderate
190°C/375°F	mark 5/mod. hot
200°C/400°F	mark 6/hot
220°C/425°F	mark 7/hot
230°C/450°F	mark 8/very hot

*For fan-assisted ovens, reduce temperatures by 10°

A BIT ABOUT THE INGREDIENTS

If you're going to splash out on a few ingredients for your store cupboard I would definitely recommend some decent vinegar, a selection of olive oils including a little bottle of truffle oil.

I always have a packet of risotto rice, barley, spaghetti and some rice noodles in my cupboards, along with some essential spices.

In my fridge there's always a piece of Parmesan and a packet of miso. I can pretty much make a meal with these basic ingredients and some veggies of course.

I thought it important to add a note about the ingredients used in this book. I do fully appreciate that some of the ingredients I've used are not always readily available in every region, but please don't stress! I've offered suitable alternatives.

MICRO SPROUTS

Micro sprouts are a favourite of mine. Different types of cress and sprouts such as shiso and coriander, are fresh, intense in flavour, colourful and perfect as garnishes. They are becoming increasingly popular in supermarkets. You could even try sprouting your own.

Micro sprouts can easily be substituted for picked herbs, but think about the final balance and just be sure they complement the flavour of the dish.

Thai basil This herb has small green leaves, purple stems and flowers, and a distinct aniseed scent and flavour. It is used as an aromatic.

Coriander Try and purchase coriander with its roots attached, as the roots have an intense flavour. Wash and store them in the freezer if you don't need them straight away. If you can't find coriander with roots, just add a few extra leaves.

ESSENTIAL ASIAN INGREDIENTS

Asian supermarkets are becoming more and more common. If you can't find one in your area, try asking your local Thai/Chinese restaurant where they buy their produce, or perhaps you could stock up online. Asian supermarkets fascinate me, I love discovering new ingredients, and here are a few of my favourite things:

Thai sweet chilli sauce One of my guilty pleasures! The Mae Ploy brand is the best, it's readily available in Asian supermarkets and I always have a bottle in my fridge.

Shoaxing Chinese rice wine, made from glutinous rice, yeast and water. It has a rich, mellow taste that enhances stir-fries and braises. Substitute with dry sherry. There are different qualities of Shoaxing available but I usually opt for the Wangzhihe and TTL brands.

Yellow Rock Sugar Looks like gem stones! Richer than granulated sugar, it's great in braises and sauces, as it gives them a beautiful glaze.

Palm sugar Palm sugar is made by boiling down the sap of palm trees. It has a creamy, rich caramel sweetness, perfect for salty sour and sweet Thai dressings; available in tubs or little discs.

Mirin Japanese sweet cooking rice wine adds sweetness to any savoury dish, substitute with sweet sherry or honey if unavailable.

VINEGARS

I'm passionate about good quality vinegars. Although they may cost a little more, they are a great way of introducing flavour.

I particularly like the Spanish Forum varieties, which are now available in the speciality aisles of supermarkets and various delis.

Chardonnay and Cabernet Sauvignon varieties are amazing and I would recommend splashing out. If you can't find them, substitute with any good red or white wine vinegar.

Balsamic increases in price with age, but that's totally understandable! If you come across anything over twelve years old it will taste like nectar! Drizzle over fresh, ripe figs with a little crumbled ricotta and a squeeze of lemon, a splash of olive oil, deeelicious!! Reduce the cheaper balsamic vinegars to a syrup for an intense flavour.

SALT

Personally I always use sea salt, my favourite's Maldon, and for pepper I like to use freshly ground black from a mill.

OLIVE OIL

It's worth investing in a few olive oils, a basic light for cooking and a fruiter richer one for dressings and drizzling. (There are some fabulous Greek varieties available.)

index

ACKNOWLEDGEMENTS

Thanks to Muna and Kyle for approaching me to write a book; it was a dream come true!

To Danielle, my editor, who has done such an amazing job of bringing my dream to life! She has listened patiently to my ideas and vision and interpreted them beautifully. With her firm but gentle support she has offered encouragement and given me motivation and inspiration when needed. But most of all she *so* understood me!

I felt so unbelievably proud and even a little emotional when Danielle sent me the first page proofs; I couldn't quite believe this beautiful book was mine! I couldn't have achieved all of this without the following people:

Jonathan Gregson – the most amazing photographer. He has bought my recipes to life with his outstanding photography. He is an inspiration and a perfectionist and so passionate about his work. As is Annie Rigg, the lovely food stylist (and her dog Mungo!). Annie has done a tremendous job preparing my recipes with exact precision. I was nervous about having someone else prepare the food, but Annie interpreted it as though I'd prepared it all myself. Thank you both for your patience, understanding and interpretation!

Thanks to Liz Belton, who read every recipe and sourced such beautiful props to complement them perfectly.

Thanks to Jane Humphrey, who has taken my vision on board and come up with this stunning design, and Anne Newman, who painstakingly checked every recipe!

Last but not least, a few personal thanks to all the chefs I've had the good fortune to work with over the last twenty years. You have been truly inspirational.

A special thank you to all the chefs who worked for me at Delfina's; it was joyous! I don't have room to name check you all, unfortunately.

To Annabelle, for patiently testing some of my recipes and to Stephanie, my mentor and friend. To Danny Boy, for your neverending support and enthusiasm: You are simply the best! To Christine Mansfield who inspired the Soft Meringue Roulade on p. 120.

Thank you to all my friends, for their enthusiasm and support for this book, and to my best friend Allison, for her endless words of encouragement and for growing such beautiful vegetables for me to experiment with!

Last but not least I thank my mum and dad for always believing in me.

Thanks to you all for making this book possible. xx